BECOMING

GLAMHAIRARTIST MEMOIR

How a Kid from Australia Became a Viral Celebrity Stylist – A True Story of Dreams, Fame, and Courage.

ATAKAN ROMANO

"From ashes to artistry, I became Glamhairartist."

Copyright

To every hand that lifted me, every eye that watched me, every heart that felt me - you are the reason Glamhairartist became eternal.

(HUDA BEAUTY Team)

From a garage salon to royal palaces, to burnout, heartbreak, and a hard reset - this is the jaw-dropping, no-filters memoir of the founder of GLAMHAIRARTIST and the exact playbook that turned virality into a second act.

ACKNOWLEDGEMENTS

I would like to express my heartfelt gratitude to the individuals and forces that have shaped not only this memoir but the very essence of my journey. Becoming Glamhairartist Atakan Romano was never the work of one person; it was the result of love, belief, mentorship, and the invisible hand of destiny guiding me every step of the way.

First and foremost, to Huda Beauty—thank you for so generously sharing my work with the world. Your reposts, encouragement, and belief in my craft were the spark that ignited my rise to virality. You gave me more than visibility; you gave me validation at a time when I needed it most. Your platform amplified my voice, and your support inspired me to push boundaries, be bolder, and dream bigger than I ever imagined. I will forever be grateful for the doors you opened, the recognition you gave, and the reminder that one act of kindness can truly transform a life.

To my father—my first and forever cheerleader. Your sacrifices, hard work, and unwavering support have been the foundation upon which every one of my successes has been built. When I doubted myself, you reminded me of my worth. When I fell, you lifted me higher. And when I soared, you stood quietly in the background, smiling, letting me shine. This book is not just my story; it is ours. Without your love and belief, none of this would have been possible.

To my family, who endured my long nights, endless hustle, and obsession with perfection—thank you for your patience, your encouragement, and for allowing me to chase a dream that often felt impossible. Every snip of the scissors, every styled strand, and every viral video carries a piece of your love within it.

To my loyal friends, clients, and followers—thank you for trusting me with your hair, your stories, and your time. You became more than clients; you became muses, partners, and believers. Every like, every share, every message of encouragement reminded me that what I was creating mattered. You turned a garage salon into a global stage.

To the industry icons and celebrities who gave me the chance to prove myself—thank you for seeing potential in a young stylist from Melbourne and allowing me to touch your hair and, in turn, your life. You didn't just give me jobs; you gave me moments that shaped my legacy.

To the haters, the critics, and those who doubted me—thank you as well. You were the fuel that made me sharper, tougher, and more determined to rise. Your doubt lit a fire in me that will never go out.

And finally, to my younger self, Emre—thank you for never letting go of the scissors, even when the world told you it wasn't possible. You dared to be different. You dared to be bold. You dared to be you. This book is proof that dreams no matter how wild can come true when you simply refuse to stop.

With deepest gratitude,

Atakan Romano

EPIGRAPH

""Fame can make you. Failure can break you.

But reinvention—reinvention is where legends are born."

Atakan Romano

DEDICATION

To the fearless dreamers who dare to hold a pair of scissors the way they hold destiny—this is for you.

The world of glam hair artistry is not just about beauty. It's about resilience, obsession, sacrifice, and vision. It's about the late nights in the salon when everyone else has gone home. It's about chasing perfection when your hands tremble, when your back aches, when your mind whispers, "You can't." And yet, you do.

I dedicate this book to every aspiring artist who looks in the mirror and wonders if they are enough. To every young stylist sweeping hair off the floor, daring to imagine that one day their name will be known. To every bold soul who has ever been laughed at for dreaming too big.

Remember this: every legend begins small. Every empire begins with a single cut, a single blow-dry, a single vision no one else could see. I, too, started at the bottom—uncertain, invisible, underestimated. They called me Emre Bardan, now known as Atakan Romano. They called me

Glamhairartist. But behind those names was a boy who refused to give up, no matter how many times the world tried to break him.

Your journey will test you. Clients will cancel. Critics will mock. Doors will slam in your face. You will bleed for your art. But in those moments, when the world tells you "no," let your passion scream louder. Let your work say what words never could.

Because artistry is not just a career—it's a calling. And if you are bold enough to answer that call, then you already belong to something greater than yourself.

Stay relentless. Stay true. Stay hungry. The glam hair world doesn't need another stylist—it needs you. Your unique eye, your fearless touch, your unapologetic brilliance. Don't dim your light to fit in—set the whole stage on fire.

I dedicate this to the next generation of artists who will carry the torch higher—to those who will look back one day and say, "I made it because I believed when nobody else did."

Keep cutting. Keep creating. Keep becoming.

Because you are not just a Glamhairartist.

You are a movement.

You are a revolution.

And the world is waiting for your crown.

CONTENTS

INTRODUCTION

In today's electrifying digital landscape, influencers seem to appear overnight, their meteoric rise painted as effortless fairytales. But my story—the story of Emre Bardan, who became Atakan Romano, the Glamhairartist— is not one of luck alone. It is a saga of scars and sparkle, of fire and rebirth. This memoir is not about stumbling into virality; it's about fighting for it with every fibre of my being, clawing my way through doubt, ridicule, and addiction, and daring to stay in the spotlight when the world tried to drag me back into the shadows.

I was born in the heart of Australia, the son of a working-class family who knew more about sacrifice than glamour. My earliest memories aren't of toys or games, but of scissors. At five years old, when most children were still learning to write their names, I was shaping hair with the seriousness of a seasoned artist. My neighbourhood became my first salon, my neighbours my first clients, and with every snip I discovered that beauty wasn't just a craft—it was my destiny.

But destiny doesn't always come wrapped in velvet. Mine was shrouded in hardship. As a boy, I dreamed of Los Angeles—the glittering runways, the celebrities, the lights. Yet I was just a kid with no money, no connections, and an accent that made me feel like an outsider. I was told "no" more times than I can count. I was laughed at, dismissed, and underestimated. But each sneer only fuelled my resolve.

Life forced me into endless survival jobs— backbreaking, joyless, consuming every ounce of energy. Eighty-hour weeks blurred into one another, yet every paycheck became a stepping stone. I saved for a rusted, broken-down car, and when I couldn't afford a salon, I transformed that car into one. The backseat became my studio, the cracked upholstery my throne. For five dollars a cut, I styled the world one client at a time. Out of that jalopy, I carved my empire.

I hustled relentlessly—sneaking onto music video sets, collaborating with local artists, and begging for opportunities others took for granted. My name began to whisper its way through the streets. Then came the night in 2017 when the universe finally listened. A single video— just me, my hands, and my vision—spread like wildfire across the internet. Overnight, millions of people saw what I had always known: I wasn't just doing hair—I was creating art. Within weeks, I had over a million followers, brand offers, and mentorships from fashion icons I had once idolized from afar.

But behind the glossy headlines was a darker truth. Viral fame brought intoxicating highs and devastating lows. Addiction wrapped its claws around me. Betrayals bruised my trust. The higher I climbed, the harder the world tried to pull me down. And yet here I stand. Reborn. Not just Emre Bardan, the boy with scissors. Not just Glamhairartist, the viral stylist. But Atakan Romano—a man forged by fire, ready to tell his story in full.

This book is not simply about hair or fame—it's about survival, reinvention, and refusing to surrender to the odds stacked against me. It's about the boy who dared to dream and the man who dared to become.

So before you turn the page, I invite you to step into my world. Witness the fire, the fall, and the rebirth. Walk with me through the shadows and into the spotlight. Because if there is one truth my journey proves, it's this: you can go viral overnight, but it takes courage, pain, and relentless passion to stay.

"Not just a child with scissors—already an artist, already a dreamer, already unstoppable."

This isn't just little Emre—aka Atakan—at five.

This is the beginning of Glamhairartist.

AUTHOR'S NOTE ON NAME & IDENTITY

This book was originally published in May 2024 under my birth name, Emre Bardan. At that time, I was still learning who I truly was—both as a person and as an artist. Since then, my journey has taken me through fire, through transformation, and ultimately, through rebirth.

Today, I stand before you as Atakan Romano. This is not a pen name, but a declaration of who I have become—a name that reflects my truth, my resilience, and the authenticity I fought to reclaim.

Every word you will read in this memoir is rooted in honesty. Where you see the name Emre Bardan, know it represents the younger version of me—the boy who dreamed, stumbled, and survived. Where you see the name Atakan Romano, know it reflects the man who rose from the ashes, reborn with clarity and purpose.

I have chosen not to erase the past, but to honor it.

This new edition is a continuation of my story—a bridge between who I was and who I am.

PROLOGUE

Reflecting on my life's journey, I can only describe it as a rollercoaster of discovery, resilience, and transformation. Born to Turkish parents, my childhood was a vibrant fusion of Turkish traditions and Australian influences. While my roots were deeply grounded in Turkish culture, it was the relaxed, creative atmosphere of Melbourne that truly shaped my outlook on life.

Although my origins trace back to Turkey, my story unfolded in the suburban heart of Australia, where I was raised in a close-knit, middle-class family. From my earliest memories, I was surrounded by warmth, affection, and encouragement—the kind of love that forms the foundation of a child's spirit. Family, after all, is the cornerstone of who we become. Yet it wasn't until I stepped into a hair salon that my true passion came alive. Within those unassuming walls, amid the rhythmic buzz of clippers and the hum of dryers, I discovered a spark that would set me on the path toward my destiny.

At the tender age of ten, I was irresistibly drawn to the world that existed behind salon doors. Although I was legally too young to work, my desire to immerse myself in hairstyling was unstoppable. I wasn't motivated by money— I simply wanted to follow my curiosity and create.

My parents, however, were firm in their opposition. They urged me to focus on my education and obey the law. Their intentions were loving and wise, yet my conviction ran deep. I knew, even then, that hairstyling wasn't just an interest—it was a calling.

Eventually, my determination softened their hearts. Seeing my passion, they allowed me to focus on learning the craft of hairdressing—cutting, styling, and colouring. That moment changed everything.

My fascination grew quickly, extending to intricate weaves and bold, vibrant dyes. The salon where I trained served more than 200 clients, and I eagerly helped with every task, from sweeping floors to cleaning after each appointment. Despite the demands, I found the work endlessly captivating and deeply fulfilling. Within just a few weeks, I had adapted effortlessly to my new role.

Looking back, even though I began working as a child, I believe it was one of the most valuable experiences of my life—a foundation that taught me discipline, creativity, and purpose.

PREFACE TO THE NEW EDITION

When I first published this memoir as Emre Bardan, it was a raw outpouring of my soul—a chronicle of struggle, addiction, ambition, and fleeting fame. I shared it as the person I was then—someone still searching for himself.

But life is a relentless teacher. Since that first edition, I have endured collapse, heartbreak, reinvention, and a spiritual awakening. The journey has reshaped not only my career but my very sense of identity.

That is why I now reintroduce this book to the world under my true name: Atakan Romano.

Within these pages, you will still meet Emre Bardan— my origin story, my former self. But you will also witness how he transformed, how pain became power, and how loss became rebirth.

To those who journeyed with me before: thank you for your loyalty and faith.

To those discovering my story for the first time: welcome to the fire, the fall, and the rebirth.

This is not merely a memoir.

This is a resurrection.

Atakan Romano.

CHAPTER 1

LOOK INSIDE

The floor tilted five degrees before anyone noticed. A thousand watts of club light burned the backs of my eyelids, and the bass hit so hard my comb skipped in my hand.

"One more," I told the girl in the chair. Then another voice, three voices, a dozen phones in the air, screens white as moons.

I had promised myself I wouldn't say yes to "just one more." But the line curled from the stage to the coat check, and every face in it shone with the kind of faith that makes you both brave and foolish. I twisted the barrel brush; the curl fell perfectly; the room blurred.

"Water," I said. The word went nowhere. The manager's hand found my shoulder. "You're good?"

I nodded because that's what professionals do. Then the club slid sideways, the floor rushed up, and the ceiling became a river of light. For a second, I thought it was smoke. It was the paramedics cutting through the crowd with their elbows, the siren singing outside, the night breathing cold on my face. I remember thinking: this is not glamorous. I remember thinking: if I don't stop, this job will stop me.

The next morning, my phone said what phones always say after a scare: bookings, DMs, a brand asking for a reel by Friday. I lay flat and watched the screen light my ceiling, feeling a kind of emptiness I didn't know hair could create. My hands—my hands—were shaking.

I used to think success was a crowded room with my name on strangers' lips. I used to pray to be reposted. I used to measure my worth by the number under my face. That's a beautiful way to begin and a terrible way to live. This book is about both.

It starts in a brick garage with a stool that wobbled and a mirror my dad drilled into a wall of crumbly mortar. It passes through salons where the air tastes like hairspray and nerves. It flies farther than I could pay for, and it wipes me

2

out in rooms I dreamed of. Then it takes me home—back to a chair, a single client, a jar where I put cash because bank apps made me anxious for a while.

I'll tell you how I got here. I'll tell you what the reposts really did, how much the tours cost, where the money went, who I disappointed, and how it felt to become a name strangers typed while I forgot mine. I'll show you the playbook I wish someone had given me before I learned it with my body. I'll tell you about the night in Monaco, yes. And I'll tell you about the morning in Melbourne when my father knocked on my door with tea and silence and saved me more than once.

If you're here for the hair, you'll get the hair. But underneath the shine is the part no camera can catch: the part where you choose whether to be a brand or a human being. I chose wrong for a while. This is how I learned to choose again.

Dear Reader,

If you've made it to this page, then you have walked with me through the untold story—the fall, and the rebirth. For that, I thank you with all my heart.

When this story was first told, I still carried the name Emre Bardan. It was the name I was born into, the name I gained fame under at sixteen, and the name that marked both my rise and my collapse. But life demanded more of me. It asked me to break, to surrender, and to transform.

Today, I stand before you as Atakan Romano—not as a mask, but as my truth. This name carries my rebirth, my strength, and my promise to never hide again.

To those who once knew me as Emre, I honor you for staying on this journey with me. To those meeting me now as Atakan, I welcome you into a story that is still unfolding.

This book is not the end. It is a beginning—a new chapter in both my life and the bond I share with you: my readers, my supporters, my family in spirit.

If this memoir touched you, inspired you, or helped you see a reflection of your own resilience, I invite you to stay connected with me. Follow my journey, join my community, and let's continue this story together beyond these pages.

4

From the ashes of Emre Bardan rose the fire of Atakan Romano. And now, together, we rise higher.

With love and gratitude,

CHAPTER 2

CHILDHOOD DREAMER; GROWING UP IN AUSTRALIA

To the rest of the world, I was just another Melbourne teen, more interested in cutting class than cutting hair. But inside our humble home, a storm was brewing—one of passion, creativity, and a fervent dream no amount of societal pressure could contain. You don't need the world's support; as long as you believe in yourself, that's enough. If you base your next move on what others expect, you're not living—you're a puppet. Live your life without seeking validation from anyone.

While other Aussie kids obsessed over football or video games, I descended from a lineage of eccentrics: a family of diehard individualists who colored outside the lines in a nation of conformity. My Muslim father recited beatnik poetry, and my artist mother longed for the bohemian energy of Melbourne's laneways. Nonconformity coursed through my veins. Our household was a kaleidoscope of clashing cultures, where the sweet scent of Buddhist incense mingled with Arabic prayers, and Sufi folk music gave way to the guttural growls of punk rock from my bedroom. In that quirky ecosystem, the only universal truth was my parents' unconditional acceptance—of me, of each other, and of anyone who walked through our door.

Being unique in a Muslim family could have been challenging, but I was lucky my parents loved me for who I was. My dad worked long hours driving trucks to support our offbeat brood, while my mum nurtured my fierce passion for hair. None of my siblings shared the same obsession, but they happily became my models, along with our pack of rescue dogs. Having supportive parents made life easier— but if your family isn't as supportive, don't be discouraged. Success is still yours to carve.

When I wasn't styling friends, I spent hours poring over magazines and exploring salons in the edgy corners of Melbourne. I clipped images, created vision boards, and studied hairstyles obsessively. To my neighbors, I was the madman roaming the streets at dawn with a garbage bag, salvaging glossy magazines from bins. At school, I was branded a "lost cause," while my peers chased varsity dreams. I craved something visceral and creative—sculpting gravity-defying hairstyles that mirrored the vivid landscapes of my imagination.

Teachers often judged me based on standardized tests, not creativity, telling me I'd never succeed. Most of them were wrong. That daydreaming rebel was quietly calculating every snip, nurturing a fiery passion that would one day make industry elites take notice.

My name is Atakan Romano, and no achievement was handed to me. I clawed my way to the top with talent, hustle, and a voracious drive to create hair-raising brilliance the world had never seen.

While other dads pushed their sons toward conventional careers, mine nurtured my spark before conformity could extinguish it. From the moment I grasped a pair of plastic scissors, Dad recognized the fire in my eyes whenever I experimented on my siblings or our rescue dogs. He ignored relatives who dismissed hairstyling as frivolous and teachers who urged more "serious" pursuits. People who tell you, "You can't," are usually projecting their own limitations.

While classmates counted down the seconds until the bell, I sketched avant-garde hairstyles inspired by rebellious icons like Nicki Minaj. Her boundary-breaking artistry became my north star.

Between school and runway editorials, my dad drove me to a grungy inner-city salon run by a kindly old-school stylist. The place smelled of hairspray and despair, but it became my sanctuary, where I absorbed technical mastery and honed my craft. Daily exposure to the scents and tools of hairstyling made me feel at home.

Dad never missed a Beat Poetry Night or PTA meeting, quietly reminding teachers that stifling creativity was akin to depriving Van Gogh of his paintbrush. With his support and motivational words from outspoken moguls, my craft evolved. I mastered braiding techniques from across the globe and pioneered cutting-edge styles that mainstream stylists lacked the audacity to attempt.

Thanks to my father's countercultural wisdom and relentless support, my formative years ignited a creative force that would erupt into a genre-defining career—one that burns as bright as the passion first stoked in my childhood.

CHAPTER 3

LATE NIGHTS, WILD CUTS, AND
HAIRSTYLING FANTASIES

The ambience of the salon felt almost surreal—so much so that I often found myself reluctant to leave, even late into the night. A young boy with a fiery passion for hairstyling was a rarity, especially one as determined as I was. Many nights, I'd walk home long after dark, though it never bothered me; our home was close enough, and the walk gave me time to dream.

On lucky days, the salon owner would offer me a lift home and sometimes a small tip. Yet amidst his generosity, he never failed to remind me that talent means nothing without relentless effort. He warned me that if I ever grew complacent, I'd lose my place in the salon. Still, beneath his sternness was respect—he saw the dedication I poured into my work and often told me so, even while expressing concern for my young age. His encouragement became a spark, one that fueled my hunger to learn and my belief that I could make something extraordinary out of this craft.

You see, in life, it's vital to have people who challenge you while believing in your potential. People come and go, but every interaction teaches us something—through both their kindness and their flaws. My time with that salon owner taught me discipline, humility, and the art of persistence. It pushed me to spend even more hours after school and on weekends perfecting my skills.

Fast forward to high school: I enrolled in a hairdressing course, defying the advice of well-meaning loved ones who urged me toward something "more practical." But I've always believed this—when you follow your passion, success or failure matters less than fulfillment. That conviction carried me through a four-year program, even as I struggled with learning difficulties.

I don't mean a literal disability, but I wasn't academically gifted. My strength was hands-on creativity, so I threw myself into mastering hairstyling while also studying hospitality and culinary arts, where I discovered another love: cooking. Remember this: focus on what you're good at, and become exceptional at it.

They say a good father is one of nature's greatest gifts, and I wholeheartedly believe it. When people ask why I speak more of my father than my mother, it's because his role in shaping my life was monumental. Having faced hardship in his own youth, he vowed to build a different future for me—to give me every chance he never had. His steadfast support became the light that guided me through uncertainty, failure, and growth.

CHAPTER 4

THE EARLY GRIND: FROM GARAGE SALON TO VIRAL VIDEOS

Opening Quote: Start small and make it big—don't let doubt stop you.

The salon's surreal atmosphere kept me lingering late into the night. A young boy with such fiery passion for hairstyling was rare—especially one like me. Walking home never bothered me; our house was close, and the quiet gave me time to dream.

On lucky nights, the salon owner would drive me home and hand me a small tip, always reminding me: work relentlessly, or you won't last here. He saw my dedication despite my age, and his tough love pushed me harder. In life, cherish those who believe in you—every person teaches you something, whether through their kindness or their flaws.

When high school came, I chose hairdressing, defying the advice of others. I've always believed that if you follow your passion, success or failure doesn't matter—you'll still find fulfillment. Despite my learning challenges (I wasn't the best academically), I threw myself into mastering hairstyling while also exploring hospitality and cooking. Focus on your strengths, and aim to become exceptional.

My father was one of life's greatest gifts—a man who vowed I'd succeed where he once struggled. His unwavering support guided me through every setback and uncertainty.

Dad even built a small salon in our garage. Within weeks, the brick-walled space was bustling, fitting five or six people at a time. I was ecstatic. Night after night, I honed my skills on synthetic hair, experimenting with secret mixes of mayonnaise, eggs, and oils that became the foundation of my revolutionary repair treatments. Using African hair products alongside my homemade formulas, I began restoring damaged hair within weeks. Watching my clients transform filled me with indescribable pride.

Of course, there were setbacks—botched colors, failed formulas, frustrated nights—but I persevered. With

Dad's unwavering faith beside me, every mistake became a lesson. Those long nights in our tiny garage were the roots of something much bigger than either of us could imagine.

My Secret Hair Repair Recipe

1. On dry hair, mix real mayonnaise with several eggs and olive oil.
2. Apply generously, cover with glad wrap, and leave for at least five to six hours—or overnight for best results.
3. Wash it off the next morning, dry your hair completely, and style as desired.

The result: stronger, shinier, healthier hair than you've ever had.

Young Atakan was in his teens when he went viral at the age of sixteen with this pencil hair tutorial.

@glamhairartist

CHAPTER 5

A STAR IS BORN: THE NIGHT THE
INTERNET EXPLODED

Opening Quote:

"You don't get to be a star without a few sleepless nights and a lot of guts."

The phone buzzed nonstop as I laid down the final curls on my latest client. Little did I know that night would change everything. A simple video, filmed on a shaky phone, would catapult me from a local hairstylist to a global sensation overnight. Suddenly, my name was everywhere—Instagram feeds, fashion blogs, even YouTube compilations.

What was the secret sauce? It wasn't luck. It was years of relentless hustle, boundless creativity, and an unshakable belief that my artistry could transcend borders. This is the story of that night when dreams collided with reality under the blinding spotlight of the digital age.

It began with a tall blonde girl who walked into my garage salon with untouched hair, model-like curves, and a quiet confidence. She'd heard whispers about my work and trusted me to transform her. Dad filmed awkwardly as I mixed products, turning her into a vision. Nervous but hopeful, I uploaded the video to Instagram and Facebook before bed.

By morning, my phone was exploding. Notifications poured in—Huda Beauty, Vegas Nay, over 500,000 shares overnight. I could hardly believe it as agents began calling.

Fame hit like a storm. My followers surged to over a million, and clients lined up around the block. But that "overnight" success was built on years of garage experiments, late-night failures, and quiet perseverance.

Shockingly, that viral moment led to my first celebrity gig—but not without doubt creeping in. Was I really ready?

Viral Quote Callout:

Viral is a moment, but mastery is a lifetime.

[Image: Full-width still from viral video, caption: "The transformation that broke the internet."]

[Image: Inset of Instagram growth chart, caption: "From 0 to 1M followers in weeks."]

Little did I know, that night was only the beginning of a wild ride filled with glamour, drama, and lessons that would test everything I believed in.

Through it all, Dad stood beside me—steady, encouraging, reminding me that resilience is the real currency of success. With renewed determination, I resolved to rise again and again, driven by the belief that greatness was never out of reach.

Atakan and his good friend Keisha—this is one of the hairstyles that went viral.

CHAPTER 6

BEYOND THE CLASSROOM, INTO THE CHAOS

*D*uring my high school years, the introduction of fashion shows added an exciting new dimension to my hairstyling journey. These events often featured collaborations with local hair academies, held either at our school or in the heart of the city.

One piece of advice from my teacher, Miss Kim, still echoes in my mind:

"It's not just about what you touch—whether it's hair, a wig, a model, or a client—it's about the passion and dedication you infuse into your work that makes it truly spectacular."

Those words became the cornerstone of my hairstyling philosophy, shaping how I approached every cut, every show, every client.

With each fashion show, I poured my heart into my craft, determined to create something unique and captivating. Recognition and praise from my teachers fueled my confidence, confirming I was on the right path. Miss Kim noticed my self-taught drive and said, "You've taught yourself everything you know." That line stayed with me for years—it was the spark that kept me going through every challenge.

While others dreamed of traditional careers, I longed for something different. I didn't want a predictable job; I wanted purpose. I envisioned a future where hairdressing wasn't just a profession but a true calling. Though moments of doubt came and went, I stayed committed to my passion, letting it guide me forward.

Hairstyling consumed me completely. The moment I held a client's hair in my hands, the rest of the world disappeared. All that remained was the canvas before me— alive, waiting to be transformed. It was exhilarating, knowing my hands could create both beauty and confidence.

Beyond the salon, I immersed myself in the pulse of the industry—studying trends, exploring new techniques, and mastering the latest innovations. As my work gained recognition, I developed a sharp eye for spotting emerging styles and making them my own. Whether experimenting with products or perfecting intricate braids, I approached each challenge with passion and persistence.

But hairstyling was never just technical—it was deeply personal. Many of my clients became more than customers; they became friends, confidantes, and sources of inspiration. I'll never forget one client who teared up after seeing her reflection. Without thinking, I started to sing to lighten the mood. My croaky voice cracked, but we both ended up laughing. That moment turned a service into a friendship, a connection that still warms my heart.

For me, hairstyling was never just about beauty—it was about making women feel like royalty. Each appointment was a chance to offer care, tenderness, and kindness, turning their hair into a crown that reflected their inner strength. In return, I gained not just loyal clients but lasting relationships built on trust and genuine connection.

With every snip of the scissors and every stroke of the brush, I found my purpose—a purpose fueled by passion, creativity, and an unwavering desire to bring out the best in every person who sat in my chair. As my journey continued, I realized this wasn't just my career; it was the essence of who I was becoming.

CHAPTER 7

VIRAL OVERNIGHT: THE FAME THAT FOUND ME

One fateful afternoon, a tall blonde woman with a round face stepped into my salon, her hair untouched by any chemical treatments. She carried herself like a model—confident, poised, and effortlessly stunning. For a moment, I was taken aback by her beauty. She had heard whispers of my work and had come to see if the rumors were true.

At the time, I had just created a new Facebook account and had only begun posting my hairstyling experiments, unsure of how the world would react. This was my chance to prove myself, and I wasn't about to waste it. Her trust ignited something fierce in me. I dove into research, hunting down the best products to suit her hair and determined to transform her into the princess she envisioned.

My father stood by, clumsily filming the process on my old phone as I worked with focused precision. Hours passed, and when I finally laid down the comb, the result was breathtaking. Her once-plain locks now shimmered with life and movement. She looked radiant—every bit the vision we had imagined together.

Still, I hesitated to share the video online. Doubt crept in. Was it good enough? But she urged me on, her voice steady and sure. "Post it," she said. "People need to see this."

That night, heart pounding, I uploaded the video to Instagram and Facebook and went to bed without expectations.

By morning, everything had changed. My phone exploded with notifications. The video had gone viral, reposted by beauty giants like Huda Beauty, Vegas Nay, and Wake Up and Makeup. Over half a million shares. Hundreds of thousands of comments. The internet had discovered me overnight.

That simple garage-salon video had become my ticket to the world stage.

Title suggestion:

GlamHairArtist: Rising to Fame with Huda Beauty's Recognition – A Teen's Journey to Becoming a World-Famous Hairstylist

CHAPTER 8

INSIDER TIPS AND TECHNIQUES
FOR ASPIRING STYLISTS

The path to becoming a celebrity hairstylist is multifaceted, encompassing education, skill development, networking, and strategic career advancement.

Foundational Education and Skill Development

*E*very great hairstylist begins with a solid foundation. The first step is education—understanding not only how to create beauty but why it works. Enrolling in an accredited cosmetology or hairdressing program provides essential training in cutting, coloring, styling, chemical treatments, and salon hygiene. But true mastery doesn't stop with a certificate.

Continuous learning is the lifeblood of this craft. Advanced workshops, seminars, and masterclasses led by industry icons sharpen technique and ignite creativity. Specialized training in editorial styling, avant-garde looks, or extensions can set a stylist apart. Just as important is understanding the language of hair itself—how different textures, from fine and straight to thick and curly, respond to tools and products. Mastering the flat iron, curling wand, diffuser, or roller is not just about usage—it's about artistry.

Building a Portfolio and Gaining Experience

A powerful portfolio is every stylist's visual resume. It tells the story of skill, versatility, and vision. Early on, offer your talents to friends, family, or aspiring models—sometimes for free—because every head of hair becomes a page in your creative journey.

Assisting established stylists, especially those with celebrity or editorial experience, provides lessons that can't be taught in classrooms. Watch, learn, and absorb how they handle clients, manage pressure, and adapt under the lights of a photoshoot or the chaos of backstage. This hands-on apprenticeship builds not just technique but confidence. Working in a reputable salon also provides structure—a place to refine your skills, earn trust, and build a loyal clientele.

Networking and Relationship Building

In this industry, talent opens the door, but relationships keep it open. Networking is more than collecting contacts; it's about cultivating genuine connections. Attend industry events, fashion shows, and beauty expos to meet photographers, makeup artists, stylists, and agents. Every handshake can lead to an opportunity.

Social media—especially Instagram—has revolutionized the beauty world. It's your digital portfolio, billboard, and business card rolled into one. Post consistently, tag brands and collaborators, and engage authentically with followers. Let your work speak before you do. And remember, professionalism matters: active listening, clear communication, and trustworthiness are what keep clients, especially celebrities, coming back.

Strategic Career Advancement

Once your foundation is built, strategy takes center stage. Seek opportunities to work on fashion campaigns, editorials, music videos, and film sets. Collaborate with rising designers and photographers—today's creative partners could be tomorrow's industry powerhouses.

Securing representation with a beauty or talent agency can open doors to larger projects and high-profile clients. Let your agent handle contracts and logistics so you can focus on your artistry. Stay ahead of trends—not just following them, but anticipating what's next. Study runway shows, pop culture, and emerging global influences.

Most importantly, develop your signature style. That's what makes a hairstylist unforgettable. In an industry built on constant reinvention, your personal brand becomes your crown—worn not just on your head, but in every masterpiece you create.

CHAPTER 9

CRAFTING A CAREER - CROWN
BY CROWN

*a*fter finishing high school, I embarked on a journey to refine my craft and carve my place in the hairstyling world. My dream was clear: to earn a position at the prestigious Toni & Guy salons in Melbourne, Australia. Known for serving the city's elite and creative class, it was the stage where the best showcased their artistry. To me, joining their team meant not only proving my skill but also stepping into the world I had envisioned since childhood—a world of style, precision, and prestige.

Working at Toni & Guy promised exposure to a diverse clientele, from the affluent to the influential. It was an opportunity to learn from the best, to challenge myself, and to see my work recognized on a larger stage.

While chasing that dream, I continued styling hair on the side, pouring my creativity into every client who sat in my chair. Each transformation—every cut, color, and contour—reminded me why I loved what I did. My reputation as a colorist began to flourish, particularly for my ability to breathe life into even the most difficult hair textures and tones. There was a unique joy in watching someone look in the mirror, fall in love with their reflection, and knowing I had a hand in that transformation.

CHAPTER 10

DUBAI DREAMS: STYLING
PRINCESSES AND BUILDING FORTUNES

*a*s I contemplated leaving the salon behind, an unexpected offer arrived—a raise. It was tempting, especially as I had begun dreaming of launching my own ventures. Yet, despite the allure of financial comfort and glamorous soirées, something kept pulling me back to the familiar rhythm of the salon—the hum of blow dryers, the laughter of colleagues, and the quiet satisfaction of creation. So, I decided to stay for another five months, dedicating myself fully while saving for the next chapter of my journey.

At nineteen, on the brink of adulthood, I received an email that would change everything: an invitation from Dubai to style the hair of a princess. Out of respect for her privacy, her name remains undisclosed, but the opportunity left me stunned. My work had somehow reached royal eyes. After confirming the offer's legitimacy, I turned to my parents for guidance. Their approval meant everything to me. Once they gave their blessing, the arrangements moved swiftly—my flight was booked, and I was set to stay in a palace hotel for eight unforgettable nights.

Arriving in Dubai felt like stepping into a dream. I was warmly welcomed and quickly immersed in work, styling one princess after another, carefully studying their hair textures and preferences. One of them smiled at her reflection and said, "Your color and design techniques are unlike anything I've seen." Her words hit me deeper than she could have known. For me, that moment was worth more than any reward.

Still, their generosity was overwhelming—lavish gifts, royal tokens, and payments that seemed unreal for someone my age. I was humbled and grateful, realizing this experience marked a turning point in my career. From the palaces of Dubai to future clients across Qatar, Kuwait, and Bahrain, my artistry had crossed borders.

When I returned to Australia, the response was electric. Clients flooded in, lining up outside my small garage salon, eager for appointments. That was when I knew it—my dream had outgrown its humble beginnings. It was time to expand.

As I reflected on my journey from the suburbs of Melbourne to the opulent suites of Dubai, I saw how passion and persistence could transform a life. Every challenge had shaped me; every opportunity had taught me resilience. Through it all, my purpose remained the same: to create beauty, empower others, and prove that dreams—even the wildest ones—are worth chasing.

CHAPTER 11

THE HUDA BEAUTY EFFECT: THE VIRAL BLESSING THAT LAUNCHED MY CAREER

Huda Kattan: From Humble Beginnings to Global Icon

Huda Kattan, the visionary behind Huda Beauty, exemplifies a journey from modest origins to worldwide acclaim. Born in Oklahoma and raised in Dubai, her multicultural upbringing instilled a deep appreciation for diversity and beauty from an early age.

Her journey began in 2010 with a simple yet powerful idea: sharing her passion for makeup through her blog, Huda

Beauty. What started as tutorials, product reviews, and honest tips soon evolved into an international platform. Her authenticity and charisma drew millions, transforming her into one of the most influential voices in beauty today.

In 2013, fueled by her entrepreneurial spirit, Huda launched her eponymous makeup brand with a single product: false eyelashes. Those lashes sold out instantly, setting the stage for what would become a billion-dollar beauty empire built on innovation, inclusivity, and empowerment. From richly pigmented palettes to cult-favorite lipsticks, every product reflected her unwavering commitment to helping people feel confident in their own skin.

The Spark That Changed Everything

When I began my hairstyling career, one quote became my mantra:

"Excellence is not an act, but a habit."

Those words guided every cut, every color, and every late night in my salon. Long before social media dominated the beauty world, I built my reputation one client at a time.

Each person who sat in my chair received more than a service—they experienced care, passion, and artistry.

Then came the moment that changed my trajectory forever.

One client, thrilled by her transformation, shared a photo of my work on her social media. At first, I didn't think much of it—until my phone began lighting up with messages. That single post ignited a chain reaction. Within days, my work was circulating across beauty pages, reaching audiences I had never imagined.

Encouraged by that client, I embraced the digital world and created my own page, @Glamhairartist. Every new post gained traction, each hairstyle spreading like wildfire. Then came the ultimate validation: Huda Beauty reposted one of my videos.

That single act changed everything.

Overnight, my work was seen by millions. My follower count skyrocketed, and opportunities began pouring in from around the world. Suddenly, I found myself traveling across continents—from Dubai's opulent suites to Istanbul's bustling salons—styling celebrities, influencers, and royalty.

Success was intoxicating, but it came with pressure. The constant expectation to outdo myself began to weigh heavily. There were nights I questioned whether I could sustain the standard I had built. Yet every challenge only strengthened my resolve. Every satisfied client reminded me why I started: to create beauty that uplifts and transforms.

The Power of a Destiny Helper

Meeting a destiny helper can feel like stumbling upon a hidden treasure—an encounter that changes everything. For me, that person was Huda Kattan.

Her decision to share my videos wasn't just an act of generosity; it was a pivotal turning point. Despite never having met, her belief in my craft unlocked possibilities I hadn't dared to imagine. Her support amplified my voice, connecting me with clients and collaborators around the globe.

With over 54 million followers on Instagram and millions more on YouTube, Huda could easily have focused solely on her empire. Yet her compassion extended far beyond business. She has always used her influence to uplift young creators, giving them visibility, encouragement, and hope.

When she shared my content, it wasn't just exposure—it was validation. Her platform became a bridge that connected my artistry to the world. That gesture, that simple act of kindness, transformed my career forever.

To this day, I remain deeply grateful. Huda didn't just help me go viral; she reminded me of the power of generosity, mentorship, and faith in others. Her spirit embodies everything I admire: brilliance, humility, and a genuine desire to see others rise.

To Huda, I offer my heartfelt thanks.

Your kindness, your belief, and your generosity changed my life.

You are proof that real success isn't just about what we build—it's about who we lift along the way.

Revamping His Best-Friend Hava's Viral Hair Tutorial: A Stylist's Touch for Internet Stardom

CHAPTER 12

A GLOBAL ADVENTURE IN
GLAM

*B*efore long, the influx of clients translated into substantial financial success—mountains of money, to be precise. It was then that I realized a childhood dream: traversing the globe. I longed to explore every corner of the world—from the icy expanses of Asia to the blazing deserts of Africa, from Europe's towering peaks to Oceania's vast oceans, and from the rainforests of South America to the frozen lands of Antarctica.

Invitations from countries around the world began pouring in, each beckoning me to showcase my hairstyling talents on international stages. Salons extended enticing offers, tempting me with lucrative salaries. Yet deep down, I nurtured a burning desire to be my own boss—to build my empire, a dream I had carried since childhood.

To manage the growing complexities of my burgeoning business, I sought a capable manager. Enter Maryam, the unsung hero behind the scenes. She deftly handled every facet of the enterprise: liaising with clients and salon owners, maintaining meticulous financial records, resolving challenges, and overseeing all logistical details— from booking international flights to coordinating appointments across continents.

Despite her preference for privacy, Maryam's unwavering dedication and strategic problem-solving proved instrumental. Under her stewardship, my business thrived for nearly six years—a period of unprecedented growth and unparalleled peace of mind. She shielded me from the distractions of online trolls and detractors, allowing me to focus entirely on my craft and brand expansion. Her eventual departure left a void no one could fill, and I often find myself reminiscing about those halcyon days of unbridled success.

By the age of nineteen, I had achieved what most could only dream of. I traveled the world, styled the hair of countless clients, and built a thriving brand recognized across continents. And yet, as much as my travels and earnings brought joy, it was the endorsement of Huda Beauty—her belief in my talent and her support in sharing my work—that had catapulted me into the spotlight and laid the foundation for everything I had accomplished.

CHAPTER 13

THE ART OF CELEBRITY STYLING:
BEHIND VELVET ROPES

*a*s I reflect on my journey in the beauty industry, one milestone stands out: the opportunity to style celebrities. It's an achievement accompanied by a whirlwind of emotions—the exhilaration of pouring your heart and soul into your craft, the satisfaction of knowing you've given it your all. Yet, a nagging doubt often creeps in, questioning whether your efforts were truly enough.

When my work gained traction on social media and went viral, it opened doors to a realm I had only dreamed of: styling the hair of the stars. Suddenly, I found myself inundated with requests from celebrities eager to experience

53

my hair-styling prowess firsthand. They spared no expense, beckoning me from near and far to receive the transformative touch that had captured the attention of countless admirers online.

Many of these luminaries already had personal hairstylists, yet they sought me out, intrigued by the possibility of something new—something different. Others sought validation, wanting to witness firsthand the authenticity of the artistry they had glimpsed through their screens.

Navigating the world of celebrity styling proved to be one of the most challenging yet rewarding aspects of my career. Each encounter brought a unique set of trials and triumphs, testing my skills and pushing me beyond my comfort zone. Yet it was precisely these challenges that fueled my passion, driving me to elevate my craft with every new opportunity.

Styling celebrities wasn't just about creating perfect hairstyles; it was a form of advertisement. Every red-carpet appearance and glamorous photoshoot served as a showcase of my talent, attracting attention and paving the way for even greater prospects.

CHAPTER 14

FROM $5 HAIRCUTS TO RED CARPET GLAM

Here, I share how I went from giving $5 haircuts to creating red-carpet glamour for celebrities and princesses in the Middle East.

The scent of cheap hairspray and the rhythmic snip of scissors were the soundtrack of my early career. I remember those days vividly—standing behind a worn-out barber chair, carefully crafting $5 haircuts in a bustling neighborhood salon. It wasn't glamorous, but it was honest work, and it taught me the fundamentals that would one day lead me into the glittering world of celebrity styling. Every precise cut and every clean fade were lessons in both technique and client satisfaction. I learned to listen not just to what a client said, but to what they truly wanted, even when their budget was limited. That experience gave me a lasting appreciation for the transformative power of a good haircut, no matter the price tag.

My journey wasn't a sudden leap; it was a steady climb, fueled by an insatiable hunger for knowledge and an unshakable belief in my artistic vision. I devoured every hair magazine, watched every tutorial, and practiced tirelessly on anyone willing to sit in my chair. I knew that to rise beyond the local salon, I had to offer more than a standard cut and style. That meant investing in myself, both creatively and financially. I saved every penny to attend advanced workshops and masterclasses, often traveling to major cities to learn from industry icons. Those early investments exposed me to new techniques, emerging trends, and a broader understanding of the global hair industry.

The Grind: Building a Foundation of Skill and Resilience

Those early years were a relentless grind. I worked long hours, often juggling multiple jobs to make ends meet while still chasing my passion for hair. I seized every opportunity—styling for local fashion shows, volunteering at community events, and saying yes to anything that could sharpen my craft. I learned the value of speed without sacrificing quality, a skill that would prove essential in the fast-paced world of celebrity styling. I also developed a keen eye for detail and a deep understanding of diverse hair textures—from fine European strands to thick, coiled African curls—which expanded my versatility as a stylist.

A pivotal turning point came when I began experimenting with editorial styling. After my regular salon shifts, I would spend hours creating intricate updos and avant-garde looks on mannequins, photographing them to build a portfolio. It wasn't about money—it was about artistic expression and pushing creative boundaries. I started reaching out to local photographers and aspiring models, offering my services for free to collaborate on projects. Those unpaid collaborations became the foundation of my unique aesthetic and helped me showcase my ability to create visually compelling, story-driven looks. That's when I began to understand the true difference between a haircut and a work of art.

Breaking Through: The First Glimmer of Glamour

My transition from local stylist to high-end professional wasn't a single breakthrough—it was a chain of interconnected opportunities. My defining moment came at a local art exhibition, where a model I had styled caught the attention of a prominent fashion editor. She took my contact information, and a few weeks later, I received a call that would change my life: an invitation to assist a renowned celebrity hairstylist on a major magazine photoshoot. The mix of exhilaration and fear was electric. This was my long-awaited entry into the world I had only imagined.

That first major shoot was a revelation. The precision, the pressure, the scale—it was a universe away from $5 haircuts. I watched everything: how the lead stylist interacted with the celebrity, how each look was planned down to the last strand. I learned about lighting, camera angles, and how to craft styles that photographed beautifully. I absorbed every lesson, every subtle detail, realizing that technical skill alone wasn't enough. Professionalism, discretion, and teamwork were just as vital.

The Ascent: From Assistant to Lead Stylist

After months of assisting and proving my dedication, I began receiving opportunities of my own. My first solo celebrity client was an up-and-coming indie musician. It wasn't a red-carpet moment, but a music video shoot with a tight budget and a demanding schedule. Still, I poured my heart into the project, creating a look that embodied her artistic vision. That success led to referrals, and slowly, my name began circulating within the industry. I made a vow to treat every client—famous or not—with the same level of care and creativity. That consistency, paired with my growing portfolio, opened doors to increasingly prestigious projects.

One of my biggest milestones came when I was hired to style hair for a major awards show. It was a true test of skill and composure. The stakes were enormous, the deadlines brutal. I planned each look meticulously, considering the outfit, theme, and personal brand of each celebrity. Seeing my work on the red carpet and across magazine covers was a deeply validating moment. It was tangible proof of how far I had come—from humble $5 haircuts to the dazzling heights of celebrity glamour.

The Middle East Connection: A New Frontier of Luxury

My entry into the Middle Eastern market was both unexpected and transformative. It began with a referral from a New York fashion editor who connected me with a client in Dubai seeking a stylist who could blend modern techniques with traditional aesthetics. The opportunity to work with royalty and high-society clientele in the region was beyond anything I had imagined. The elaborate events, the cultural nuances, and the demand for perfection presented both challenges and creative inspiration.

Working with Middle Eastern royalty required not just artistry but cultural sensitivity and discretion. I immersed myself in learning about traditional hairstyles, accessories, and local preferences. The focus on elegance, modesty, and intricate detailing pushed me to innovate while respecting cultural heritage. Blending contemporary trends with timeless beauty became my hallmark. The grandeur of these occasions—from opulent weddings to royal ceremonies—was breathtaking, and being part of such artistry was an immense privilege.

The Art of Transformation: Beyond the Hair

If there's one truth my journey has taught me, it's that hairstyling is far more than cutting and coloring—it's transformation. It's understanding who someone is and reflecting that identity through style. Whether it was a client preparing for a job interview or a celebrity walking the red carpet, each sought transformation. The tools may have evolved, and the budgets may have grown, but the desire to feel one's best remains unchanged. That understanding has guided my entire career, allowing me to connect with people on a deeper, more human level.

From the humblest beginnings in a local salon to the shimmering lights of red carpets and royal palaces, my story is a testament to perseverance, passion, and lifelong learning. The $5 haircuts taught me humility and precision; the red carpets taught me artistry and excellence. Every step of the way, I've carried forward the same belief that with dedication and purpose, anything is possible. This isn't just a story about hair—it's a story about transformation, one strand at a time.

CHAPTER 15

IMAGINATIVE INNOVATIONS: CREATING VIRAL HAIRSTYLES THAT SHOCKED THE WORLD (gallery of pics for this one to be added)

Tegan Martin, crowned Miss Universe Australia, relied on the expertise of Glamhairartist for her stunning hairdo.

CHAPTER 16

CELEBRITY ENCOUNTERS: NOTABLE NAMES IN GLAMHAIRARTIST'S PORTFOLIO

The Stars Who Shaped My Career — and the Scandals That Rocked It

Opening Quote: Every client is a canvas; every style, a story.

Fame eventually brought some of the world's most celebrated figures to my chair, but not without its fair share of drama.

In Istanbul, I styled the luminous Nez Demir, whose 3.7 million followers and effortlessly silky hair made her a beauty icon. Working with her was more than a professional milestone; her philanthropy and authenticity were a constant source of inspiration.

Then came Mona Kattan — entrepreneur, @Kayali founder, and sister to Huda Kattan — whose regal elegance defined the Dubai beauty scene. Crafting looks for her was a masterclass in blending sophistication with glamour.

Çağatay Akman, the soulful singer, became both a client and a friend: always humble, always grounded, even amid fame. Semih Varol, a 2.7-million-follower influencer, embraced bold, unconventional color choices that reflected his vibrant personality.

Actress Bestemsu Özdemir, known for her role in Muhteşem Yüzyıl (Magnificent Century), challenged me to transform her look for each new character, while Gamze Özçelik, beloved TV star and philanthropist with 1.5 million followers, radiated warmth and grace in every session.

For Burcu Güneş, the rising singer, I designed elegant layers that complemented her stage presence. With the legendary Sezen Aksu, the "Queen of Turkish Pop," our sessions often turned emotional — she carried a rare creative spirit that filled the room.

My journey also took me beyond Turkey: Janet Roach from The Real Housewives franchise and Chloe Ortac, model and influencer, brought energy and glamour to every chair. Zeynep Ilıcalı, a renowned businesswoman, experienced a stunning transformation under my hands, while Reem Erhama, the celebrated Bahraini actress, became a recurring client during my sessions across the UAE.

Each name added a new dimension to my craft — proof that even behind the world's brightest stars, the artistry of hair remains a deeply human connection.

Glamhairartist worked his magic on Mona Kattan's hair, following in the footsteps of her sister Huda, who catapulted Glam to internet stardom. The transformation was simply incredible.

@glamhairartist

CHAPTER 17

DAPHNE JOY: CRAFTING A
GODDESS CROWN FROM
HOLLYWOOD

Daphne Joy: A Beacon of Beauty, Talent, and Influence

*D*aphne Joy stands as a beacon of beauty, talent, and influence in the realms of modeling, acting, and social media. Born on February 8, 1987, in Olongapo, Philippines, she has captivated audiences worldwide with her striking presence and remarkable versatility.

As a model, Daphne has graced countless fashion campaigns, magazine covers, and runways, commanding attention with her undeniable confidence and allure. Her transition into acting further revealed her multifaceted talents, earning her memorable roles in both film and television.

In the illustrious world of beauty and glamour, Atakan Romano — the prodigious hairstylist known as Glamhairartist — reigns supreme, once more setting hearts aflutter with his latest masterpiece: a stunning look for the captivating Daphne Joy, the former wife of rap legend 50 Cent, created for a prestigious gala event.

Atakan's journey into hairstyling began at the tender age of thirteen, when his nimble fingers first wielded scissors and combs with the precision of a natural artist. Driven by an insatiable passion for his craft, he embarked on a global journey, traversing continents, mastering techniques, and building a reputation as one of the most visionary hairstylists in the industry.

His rise to international prominence came through the power of digital media: a viral hair video that captured the imagination of beauty enthusiasts worldwide and led to an invitation to showcase his artistry amid the opulence of Dubai's elite beauty scene.

Today, Atakan stands as a paragon of creativity and innovation, his name synonymous with hairstyling brilliance and luxury artistry. For the gala event graced by Daphne Joy, he drew upon both contemporary trends and his boundless imagination to create a look that epitomized sophistication and daring elegance — a symphony of style that highlighted Daphne's natural radiance.

The world took notice as his creation dazzled across social platforms, igniting admiration and acclaim from fans and professionals alike. With every stroke of his brush and each meticulous twist of his fingers, Atakan reaffirmed his status as a true trailblazer — an artist whose work transcends hairstyling to become a celebration of beauty and self-expression.

As the curtain falls on yet another triumph for Glamhairartist, anticipation builds for the next chapter in Atakan's extraordinary career. With his unmatched talent, passion, and dedication, his legacy in the world of beauty continues to grow, destined to be etched in the annals of hairstyling history.

Daphne's personal life has also drawn public attention, particularly her past relationship with rapper 50 Cent. Together, they share a son, Sire Jackson, born in 2012.

Though their romantic relationship ended, Daphne and 50 Cent maintain a positive co-parenting relationship, placing their son's well-being above all else.

Beyond her professional achievements, Daphne has become a powerful voice in the digital space. Her vibrant presence on social media, especially on Instagram, has solidified her as a sought-after influencer. Through curated glimpses into her life, fashion, and beauty routines, she continues to captivate followers with authenticity and style.

When the opportunity arose to style Daphne's hair, I embraced it with enthusiasm. Initially, I considered a technique tailored to her silky texture, but instinct guided me toward a bolder approach. During our session, a phone call between Daphne and her then-husband, 50 Cent, hinted at personal challenges, yet she remained composed and graceful. I focused on creating a glamorous, voluminous blowout that emphasized her striking features and exuded confident allure.

The finished look embodied a seamless fusion of classic and modern elements, leaving a lasting impression on both Daphne and everyone who saw it. When I shared the image online, it quickly drew attention and admiration, with countless followers requesting the same style.

Although based in the United States, Daphne continues to seek my expertise whenever she visits Turkey. Our ongoing collaboration stands as a testament to the trust she places in my artistry and to the transformative power of a beautifully crafted hairstyle.

Each opportunity to work with Daphne Joy reignites my passion for hairstyling and deepens my commitment to excellence. Together, we create more than looks — we create moments of beauty and confidence that linger far beyond the salon chair.

CHAPTER 18

CARLA DIBELLO: THE BUSINESS OF BEAUTY & POWER BEHIND THE SCENES

Carla DiBello: A Bold Hair Transformation

Carla DiBello, the esteemed television producer and entrepreneur, reached out to me seeking a hair transformation that would reflect her vibrant, fearless personality. Over the phone, we discussed her vision in detail, and I carefully analyzed her hair to determine the best approach. Employing an innovative technique, I set out to craft a look that would defy convention and make a bold statement — an asymmetrical cut that read edgy, dynamic, and unapologetically modern. The finished style challenged tradition and announced Carla's adventurous spirit. It also marked a moment that helped establish my reputation for pushing boundaries in the world of hairstyling. At the time of our collaboration, Carla also served as Kim Kardashian's manager, adding another layer of significance to our work together.

Atakan Romano Becomes Personal Hairstylist to Carla DiBello

Step into the world of celebrity style with Atakan Romano, a hairstylist whose mastery continues to attract the most illustrious names in Hollywood. My latest venture brought me into Carla DiBello's inner circle — an opportunity to sculpt looks that redefine elegance, sophistication, and red-carpet allure. From Beverly Hills fittings to star-studded events, our partnership was built on mutual trust, creative risk-taking, and an uncompromising commitment to perfection.

As Carla's personal hairstylist, I approached each transformation as a collaborative act of styling and storytelling. Every strand was placed with intent; every curl and fall was chosen to complement her presence and the image she wanted to project. Beyond the glossy surface of

celebrity, our bond grew from a shared creative language —
a partnership where beauty became an expression of inner
strength, confidence, and identity.

The Mastery Behind the Look

When Carla arrived, her hair was thick, dyed black,
and heavily processed. She told me simply: "Do whatever
you think suits me — turn this into magic." I assessed her
hair, skin tone, and facial structure, then made a plan: a
metallic, crystal-grey tone built on carefully executed
lightening and intensive protection.

Bleaching a previously black-dyed mane is a
multistage process with risks if not handled correctly. I
lightened her hair progressively, using protective protocols
and restorative treatments after each session to maintain
integrity. On the second day, we repeated the lightening with
caution and continued deep-conditioning treatments. I then
applied my signature metallic grey blend using professional
lines such as Fanola and Affinage, layering pigments until
the precise shade matched my vision. I followed with blue-
toned shampoos and prolonged treatments to lock in colour
and strengthen the hair.

Styling was the final flourish. After a meticulous blowout with heat protection, I created soft waves with curling tongs to maximize movement and shine. The transformation was dramatic. Carla loved it — she was obsessed. I also walked her through a detailed aftercare routine to ensure the colour would remain luminous and her hair healthy.

When I posted the result online, the response was immediate. The look went viral, was widely reshared, and created demand from clients across the Middle East and beyond. Because the process required multiple sessions and careful maintenance, clients commissioned the full transformation as a multiday service. I priced bespoke transformations in the premium range of my services accordingly. The priority throughout was never speed but safety, ensuring hair remained healthy while delivering a princess-like finish.

Masterclass: Insider Tips & Techniques

Excellence is a habit. For stylists who want to replicate elements of this transformation, the essentials are: assess the client's history and hair health; plan a staged lightening protocol; protect and repair between sessions; choose pigments that layer well; and commit to meticulous aftercare. My custom "Crystal Grey" signature requires precise mixing, multiple colour applications, and targeted treatments to maintain shine, tone, and strength. Film your process for social platforms — well-shot reels have brought my work to a global audience.

Final Note

This collaboration with Carla DiBello reinforced something I've long believed: great transformations are equal parts technical skill, creative vision, and care. When you combine those elements, you don't just change hair — you create confidence.

CHAPTER 19

IMAGINATIVE INNOVATIONS:
CREATING VIRAL HAIRSTYLES
THAT SHOCKED THE WORLD

If there's one thing nature blessed me with, it's a boundless imagination.

While I wouldn't call myself a magician, I've never struggled to conjure innovative hairstyling techniques.

What truly set me apart from the millions of hairstylists around the world was my creative flair it gave me the freedom to envision endless designs, colour combinations, and techniques.

Among my many creations, one of my proudest was a distinctive blend: deep dark brown roots melting seamlessly into a dreamy blonde.

I've always had a soft spot for vibrant, colourful hair, often working with Manic Panic's Unicorn Colours.

Their spectrum of hues allowed me to craft mesmerizing rainbow tones that radiated beauty and individuality.

A friend once told me my designs looked almost magical and asked where my inspiration came from.

I explained that I've always been drawn to the impossible exploring the unknown and embracing the new.

What might seem complex to others, like my intricate rainbow colouring, came naturally to me a reflection of both my creativity and skill.

One of my signature techniques eventually went viral, thanks to the incredible support of Huda Beauty, who showcased my work across her social media channels.

That moment marked a turning point, cementing my online identity as Glamhairartist and propelling me into the global spotlight.

Soon, hairstylists from all over the world began recreating my look and tagging me with #dreamhairwithme.

My portfolio soon became a tapestry of artistry from classic Hollywood curls and elegant waves to daring blowouts.

Each style told a story, each transformation reflected my dedication to turning a client's dream into reality.

Their joy and confidence after each session became the most rewarding part of my craft.

The recognition extended beyond social media, leading to numerous interviews on air in both Turkey and Australia.

Journalists often asked about my motivation and vision as a creative hairstylist.

I shared my belief in pushing artistic boundaries, experimenting fearlessly, and celebrating individuality through design.

My mission has always been to leave a lasting imprint on the world of hair artistry inspiring others to dream boldly, create passionately, and redefine what beauty can be.

CHAPTER 20

DISASTER IN MONACO NEAR-
DEATH EXPERIENCE

Something truly frightening happened to me—an experience I'll never forget.

It was one of those moments that reminds you just how fragile life is and how quickly everything can shift.

It all began with an invitation to a major hair event in Monaco. When the message came, I wasn't sure I wanted to go. My schedule was overflowing, and rest had become a luxury I couldn't seem to afford. But my manager insisted it would be an incredible networking opportunity, so I reluctantly agreed.

When we arrived, Monaco was even more extravagant than I'd imagined. The party took place at a glamorous nightclub near the legendary Monte Carlo Casino. Lights shimmered. Champagne flowed endlessly. The room buzzed with electricity. I never expected so many people would be there, all eager for me to style their hair.

As a celebrity hairstylist, I'm used to attention—just not this level of it. One client after another lined up, and I kept working nonstop, determined to keep up with the demand. Hours passed. The music pounded through the walls. My vision blurred, and my head felt light, but I pushed on. Then, without warning, everything went black.

When I woke up, I was in a hospital bed—disoriented, weak, and surrounded by harsh white light. The doctor explained I had collapsed from exhaustion and dehydration. If the medical team hadn't acted quickly, things could have ended very differently.

My manager never left my side. As soon as I was cleared to leave, she insisted we get out of Monaco immediately. She didn't want to take another chance with my health—and honestly, neither did I.

That experience was a wake-up call. In chasing success, I'd forgotten to care for the person behind the brand—me. I had been so focused on building my name and career that I neglected the simplest, most vital thing: taking care of my body.

As we drove away from Monaco, gratitude washed over me—gratitude for my manager's loyalty, for the doctors who saved me, and for the reminder that life is far more important than any milestone on my résumé.

Looking back now, I'm proud of what I've achieved: creating transformative hairstyles, empowering clients, and using my platform to uplift marginalized voices. But above all, I've learned that success means nothing without health. That lesson didn't just change the way I work—it changed the way I live.

The Monaco Bathroom Floor

The marble was cold against my cheek—imported Italian Carrara, probably costing more per square foot than most people made in a month. But at 4:17 a.m. on September 23, 2014, as consciousness flickered like a dying bulb, all I could think was how ironic it would be to die surrounded by luxury that meant absolutely nothing.

The Setup: Paradise as Prison

Monaco in July is breathtaking—the kind of beauty that explains why billionaires choose to live there. The Mediterranean shimmered like liquid diamonds, the architecture blended old-world elegance with modern sophistication, and the entire principality felt like a movie set designed to showcase wealth.

I'd been invited to style three clients for events that would be photographed by international media and seen by millions. The offer seemed irresistible: €200,000 for three sessions over four days, first-class accommodations at the Hotel Hermitage, and introductions to European aristocrats and American tech moguls.

But what looked like the pinnacle of success quickly became a velvet-lined prison. The pressure to perform flawlessly for clients whose reputations depended on perfection was suffocating. Paparazzi lurked everywhere, amplifying the anxiety. And being in a foreign country where I knew no one—and barely spoke the language— magnified every internal struggle I'd been carrying.

The Clients: When Perfection Isn't Optional

The first client, Countess Antonia—an Italian textile heiress—needed to be flawless for a charity gala attended by Prince Albert, European royalty, and billionaires whose combined wealth rivalled that of small nations.

"I need to look like I was born for this moment," she said. "But in a way that doesn't look like I tried. Effortless elegance—that's the only acceptable aesthetic here."

Creating an "effortless" look that required hours of meticulous colour work and precision styling was a paradox I knew well, but never with stakes this high. One misstep could damage multimillion-euro relationships and shut me out of the luxury market forever.

Six hours of colour blending. Custom formulas tailored to her tone and lighting. Triple conditioning treatments. An exacting cut. Every move designed to photograph flawlessly from every angle.

The Pharmaceutical Escalation

The perfect storm of exhaustion, pressure, and isolation made my usual medication routine useless. Adderall no longer sharpened my focus; Xanax barely touched the panic of being constantly watched.

So I escalated—doubling stimulant doses, mixing benzodiazepines, adding muscle relaxants and beta-blockers to steady my hands and heart. The combinations created alternating waves of euphoria and numbness, but they worked. I could perform for eighteen straight hours—sharp, charming, technically flawless—even if the process was slowly killing me.

The Warning Signs

By day three, the signs were undeniable: trembling hands, dilated pupils, slurred or erratic speech, stumbling coordination. Anyone in medicine would have recognized toxicity, but in the beauty world, this level of strain was romanticized—passion mistaken for dedication. Clients saw my shaking hands as excitement. Management called it artistic intensity.

The Third Client: Breaking Point

Lady Catherine Pemberton was different—warm, perceptive, genuinely kind.

"Darling," she said, "you look dreadful. When did you last sleep or eat properly? You can't keep this up."

Her concern nearly broke me. It was the first moment of human empathy I'd felt in weeks, and it revealed just how fragile I had become. I completed her session flawlessly, but inside I felt hollow—like a machine executing creativity without emotion.

The drugs that once enhanced brilliance were now impersonating it.

The Breaking Point: When Enhancement Becomes Poison

The final evening should have been triumphant: three flawless sessions, elite clients, and promises of future work. Instead, everything felt empty. When the medications stopped working as before, I escalated again—layering stimulants with depressants, painkillers, sleep aids, and supplements in a frantic attempt to feel "balanced."

I was trying to chemically engineer calm, focus, and joy at the same time. Instead, I created chaos.

The Near-Death Experience

The overdose came fast—hallucinations, visual distortions, respiratory failure. The marble walls seemed to breathe, the lights pulsed in geometric patterns, and my reflection in the mirror morphed into a stranger.

Breathing became a conscious effort—each inhale a decision that grew harder to make. When it hit me that I was dying, I also realized just how much I wanted to live.

Voices—real or imagined—echoed through the hallucinations: dead relatives, disappointed clients, critics that lived in my head. All repeating the same truth: I had built my success on performance, not presence.

The Physical Crisis

When Lady Catherine couldn't reach me, she sent hotel staff to check my room. They found me unresponsive on the bathroom floor. The hotel's medical team acted quickly, though even they struggled to identify what I'd taken. My drug cocktail was improvised chaos—no dosage, no logic, no limits.

The Aftermath: Survival and Reckoning

My physical recovery was fast. The emotional and professional recovery took years. Explaining what happened without destroying my career felt impossible. Admitting the truth meant risking everything; hiding it meant returning to the lie that nearly killed me.

I learned the hard way that performance enhancement always follows a tragic arc: helpful becomes necessary, and necessary becomes dangerous.

The Monaco Lesson

That marble floor taught me the cost of deception—yes, to others, but more importantly to myself. I built a career on perfection that demanded I be chemically perfect too. But perfection built on poison cannot last.

I didn't die in Monaco. But the person who woke up in that hospital bed wasn't the same one who checked into the Hotel Hermitage.

CHAPTER 21

THE STORM OF HEARTBREAK: WHEN GLAM FELL APART

Following the Monaco incident, my manager urged me to step back from the spotlight—a decision that weighed heavily on me despite the success, wealth, and recognition I had achieved. She emphasized the importance of taking a meaningful break to prioritize my mental and emotional health, and perhaps to explore new avenues of purpose beyond the salon.

Reluctantly, I agreed. I stepped away from hairstyling, intending to return after a short pause—though that comeback never truly happened.

It was during one of my quiet visits to the salon, long after I had slowed down, that I met someone who would leave an indelible mark on my life. She carried herself with warmth and grace—kind, intelligent, and supportive. For the first two or three years, her presence became my greatest source of motivation. Together, we built memories that felt straight out of a dream: spontaneous adventures, shared laughter, and tranquil boat cruises that remain among my most cherished moments. I felt lucky to have found someone who not only believed in my vision but also walked beside me as I rediscovered my sense of self.

But the fairytale didn't last. My dream of building a loving home and nurturing a family was shattered by a painful breakup that left me questioning everything I thought I knew about love and loyalty.

In the months that followed, I turned inward, searching for peace through healing, forgiveness, and growth. My aspirations of leaving a legacy for future generations suddenly felt uncertain—replaced by the quiet struggle of rebuilding from heartbreak.

The question of why still lingers in many minds, and I understand that curiosity. "Love can make you or mar you," my manager once told me—words that echo louder now than ever. I held on, hoping for change, but the relationship drained more from me than it gave. Slowly, my drive faded, my passion dimmed, and my career momentum began to stall under the weight of emotional exhaustion.

Yet even in that darkness, I began to rediscover something essential—myself.

CHAPTER 22

❧ ❧ ❧

GLOBAL ADVENTURES: TOURS, TRANSFORMATIONS & TRIUMPHS

The Genesis of Glam: A Small-Town Dreamer with Big-City Ambitions

The story begins not in a bustling metropolis but in a quiet, often overlooked hometown. Our protagonist—a young, imaginative aspiring hair artist—discovers an innate fascination with beauty and transformation. Early inspirations bloom from the delicate scent of a grandmother's vanity table, the glossy pages of fashion magazines, and the laughter of friends and family who unknowingly became the first "clients."

These humble beginnings ignite the spark of a lifelong passion. Through small triumphs and inevitable stumbles—the first haircut that went right, the long nights of practice, the doubts that whispered in the background—resilience begins to take form. Then comes a defining moment: a local competition, a chance encounter with a visiting stylist, or the sudden realization that the hometown scene can no longer contain such growing ambition. This becomes the catalyst for the first bold leap—leaving behind the familiar to chase a dream in a larger city.

From Salon Floors to International Shores: The Call of the Global Stage

The journey continues in a major fashion hub—perhaps New York, London, or Paris—where ambition collides with reality. The protagonist faces grueling hours, exacting mentors, and the whirlwind chaos of high-fashion hairstyling. Backstage at Fashion Week and at celebrity events, every challenge evolves into a lesson in artistry and endurance.

This is where the "tours" begin—first as a member of a creative team, then as a recognized talent. The experiences are electric: the adrenaline of runway shows, the pressure of last-minute fixes, and the joy of seeing one's work in magazines and on screens across the world. The global exposure sharpens skill while revealing the boundless energy of cultural diversity—a force that steadily shapes a unique creative identity.

The Art of Adaptation: Navigating Diverse Cultures and Hair Textures

As recognition grows, solo adventures take flight. Each international assignment brings new lessons and unexpected challenges. The artist learns to adapt—to local hair textures, beauty ideals, and customs—while remaining rooted in authenticity. From navigating language barriers to forging creative collaborations, every encounter becomes a cultural exchange.

Vivid memories surface: a spontaneous styling session in Tokyo, a desert photoshoot in Dubai, a heartfelt moment shared with a client in Rio. These experiences deepen both artistry and empathy, revealing beauty as a universal language that transcends borders.

Transformations Beyond the Chair: Personal Growth Through Global Encounters

The narrative turns inward, exploring how travel and creativity intertwine to shape personal growth. Homesickness, self-doubt, and culture shock slowly give way to discovery, courage, and gratitude. Each challenge—whether a misstep in a foreign salon or a night of introspection abroad—becomes part of a larger transformation.

Through these moments, the protagonist learns that success is defined not only by accolades or fame, but by the quiet confidence of knowing one's purpose. Global encounters nurture wisdom, humility, and an ever-evolving artistic soul.

Triumphs and Legacy: Giving Back and Inspiring the Next Generation

The journey reaches its crescendo—success achieved, lessons learned, and gratitude overflowing. The artist, now known as Glamhairartist, channels years of experience into something greater than personal recognition: legacy.

Whether opening international salons, mentoring rising stylists, or advocating for diversity and inclusion, every effort reflects a commitment to uplift others. Workshops in underserved communities, collaborations with young creatives, and initiatives that champion self-expression all reinforce a central truth: beauty has the power to transform lives.

The memoir closes not as an ending, but as a continuation—a reminder that passion, perseverance, and purpose can turn even the smallest dreams into global triumphs.

CHAPTER 23

BUILD YOUR EMPIRE IN 5 STEPS

*M*y journey didn't begin with a perfectly coiffed client but with a tangled mess of dreams and a fierce desire to create. I was a young stylist fresh out of cosmetology school, armed with a diploma and a head full of ambition. The salon floor felt like a battlefield—each snip and style a skirmish against self-doubt and the relentless pursuit of perfection.

I remember those early days vividly—the long hours, the aching feet, and the constant hustle to build a clientele from nothing. It wasn't glamorous; it was pure grit. I watched other stylists effortlessly fill their books, their social feeds buzzing with engagement and admiration. I wanted that. I craved that connection—not just to transform hair, but to transform lives.

This memoir isn't merely my story. It's a roadmap for every aspiring hair artist who dreams of turning passion into a thriving empire, one viral post at a time. True success isn't built on talent alone; it demands strategy, resilience, and a touch of digital magic.

This is the story of Becoming Glamhairartist.

Chapter 1 — The Foundation: Mastering Your Craft and Finding Your Niche

Before you can build an empire, you must first build your foundation. For me, that meant relentless dedication to mastering my craft. I spent countless hours practicing, attending workshops, and absorbing every bit of knowledge I could find.

Technical proficiency is non-negotiable—you can't fake good hair. This stage was about understanding color theory, refining cutting techniques, and developing an instinct for what truly flatters a client. It was also about discovering my artistic identity. What made my heart race? What kind of beauty did I want to bring into the world?

For me, it was vibrant, transformative color and intricate, elegant updos. Choosing a specialty wasn't just creative—it was strategic. In a crowded market, generalists fade into the background. As marketing expert Seth Godin says, "Specialization is the key to differentiation." By carving out a niche, I positioned myself as the go-to stylist for clients seeking something distinctively mine.

I documented everything—even my imperfect attempts—knowing that growth thrives in vulnerability. Every critique and correction became a stepping stone. Those unseen hours of practice became the foundation for everything that followed.

Chapter 2 — The Digital Launchpad: Building Your Online Presence

Once my hands were steady and my style defined, it was time to step onto the digital stage. This wasn't about posting pretty pictures; it was about building a brand.

I began with Instagram—the visual playground for modern hair artists. I focused on quality over quantity: clean lighting, sharp photography, and captions that revealed the story behind each transformation. It wasn't just "before and after"; it was emotion, confidence, and connection.

Hashtags became my discovery engine. As digital strategist Neil Patel notes, "Hashtags act as a discovery tool, allowing users to find content related to their interests." Through smart tagging and consistent posting, my audience grew organically.

I also created a simple, professional website on Squarespace—a digital home that showcased my portfolio, pricing, and booking details. It elevated my credibility and streamlined the client experience.

The key lesson? Your online presence should feel like an extension of your artistry—curated, authentic, and unmistakably you.

Chapter 3 — The Virality Code: Creating Content That Captivates and Converts

Skill alone doesn't build momentum; storytelling does. To stand out, I needed content that stopped the scroll and sparked connection. My strategy centered on five content pillars:

1. Education: I created short tutorials like "How to Achieve Perfect Beach Waves" and "Maintaining Vibrant Hair Color at Home." Teaching built trust—and trust built clients.

2. Behind the Scenes: Authenticity fosters connection. Sharing snippets of salon life, challenges, and triumphs made my audience feel part of the journey.

3. Client Transformations: Real people, real joy—that's the magic. Testimonials and videos spoke louder than any ad campaign.

4. Trend Spotting: Highlighting new techniques and color innovations positioned me as an industry leader.

5. Interactive Engagement: Polls, Q&As, and challenges turned my followers into an active, engaged community.

Then came short-form video. TikTok became my creative playground, where I learned the art of concise, visually striking storytelling. Consistency proved crucial; as Hootsuite advises, "Regular posting keeps your audience engaged and signals relevance to algorithms."

I built a content calendar, stayed organized, and treated my feed like a gallery—every post intentional, every caption purposeful.

Chapter 4 — The Growth Engine: Analytics and Community Building

Going viral is exhilarating, but sustaining growth is the true test. I dove deep into analytics, studying what resonated—colors, captions, formats, and posting times. As HubSpot reminds us, "Understanding audience behavior through analytics is essential for optimization."

But numbers only tell part of the story. Real growth comes from real connection. I replied to every comment, every DM, every tag. I collaborated with local brands, partnered with influencers, and hosted virtual workshops.

That's when I learned one of the most valuable lessons of all: a thriving community isn't built on followers; it's built on relationships. My clients and followers weren't just supporters—they were advocates who carried my brand into spaces I could never reach alone.

Chapter 5 — The Empire Blueprint: Monetization and Scaling Your Success

With influence comes opportunity—and the ability to turn creativity into sustainability. I diversified my income streams with intention:

1. Premium Services: I refined my offerings, introduced personalized experiences, and priced my expertise confidently.
2. Online Education: I launched digital courses and guides through Teachable, sharing my techniques with stylists worldwide.
3. Affiliate Partnerships: I collaborated with trusted brands, recommending only products I truly believed in—turning authenticity into revenue.
4. Brand Collaborations: Sponsored campaigns and industry partnerships amplified my reach.
5. Mentorship: Coaching aspiring stylists became a way to give back, helping others find their voice in a competitive industry.

The path from struggling stylist to Glamhairartist wasn't easy—it was built through countless hours of persistence, creativity, and unwavering belief.

By mastering my craft, building a digital identity, creating captivating content, studying analytics, and scaling strategically, I transformed a passion into a global brand.

This memoir is not just my reflection—it's proof that with vision, courage, and digital savvy, you can turn artistry into legacy.

CHAPTER 24

CRYSTAL GREY 40K$: THE
SIGNATURE SHADE THAT CHANGED
EVERYTHING

Atakan's forthcoming book promises a captivating exploration of the artistry behind crafting the coveted crystal grey hair color. Anticipate its release with bated breath! Let's dive in.

*D*reams to Dollars: The Unstoppable Rise of Glamhairartist" immerses readers in the awe-inspiring journey of a true luminary in the hairstyling world.

Prepare to be swept away as you explore "From Local Braiding to $40k Signature Style: The Viral Odyssey of Glamhairartist." This riveting narrative unveils the extraordinary transformation of a young visionary who defied all odds to claim his place among the stars.

Experience the electrifying story of how a single viral hair tutorial ignited a global sensation, propelling a teenage prodigy into the stratosphere of hairdressing greatness.

Through vivid, gripping prose, Atakan Romano's story leaps off the page, transporting you from humble beginnings to the dizzying heights of international acclaim. Witness firsthand the meteoric ascent of a true icon in the making. With each turn of the page, you'll be captivated by Emre's unwavering commitment to his craft and inspired by his relentless pursuit of excellence.

"Dreams to Dollars" is more than a book – it's an invitation to dream bigger, reach higher, and unleash the unstoppable force of your own potential.

Prepare to be inspired, enthralled, and empowered. Emre Bardan's story stands as a testament to the transformative power of passion and the boundless possibilities awaiting those brave enough to chase their dreams.

Don't miss this extraordinary journey. Pre-order your copy of "Dreams to Dollars" today and embark on an adventure that will leave you forever changed.

The Spark: The Unconventional Client and the "Crystal Grey" Experiment

Every great breakthrough begins with a risk—and for Alex, it came in the form of an unconventional client. She was fearless, artistic, and unapologetically bold.

"I want something no one else has," she said, her voice charged with both trust and challenge. That single sentence would change everything.

For Alex, the request ignited a creative storm. He saw in it not just a hairstyle, but a statement—a chance to redefine beauty itself. Late nights in the salon became experiments in alchemy: silver, ash, lavender, blue—each pigment carefully measured and remixed in pursuit of perfection. The air was heavy with the scent of developer and determination.

"Crystal Grey" wasn't born from a bottle; it was engineered from instinct, science, and soul. It required an intuitive understanding of light, tone, and texture—of how

117

color interacts with emotion. Each test strand shimmered with potential until, finally, the formula revealed itself: a luminous, cool-toned grey kissed with subtle violet undertones, shifting like glass under sunlight.

When the color was revealed, the client's eyes widened. Her reflection glowed—sophisticated yet otherworldly.

"It's magic," she whispered.

And in that moment, Crystal Grey came to life—not just as a color, but as a revolution.

The Viral Sensation: From Salon Chair to Global Phenomenon

The next morning, the client posted a photo of her new look. Within hours, the internet caught fire. Likes, shares, and comments poured in—first from friends, then strangers, and soon from influencers across continents.

"Who did this color?" became the question on everyone's feed.

By the week's end, Alex's phone was vibrating non-stop. Bookings poured in. Reporters called. Celebrities sent direct messages. Everyone wanted Crystal Grey.

The sudden fame was exhilarating—and overwhelming. The salon transformed overnight into a creative battleground. Each client expected magic, and Alex delivered, fueled by equal parts adrenaline and artistry. Behind the glamour, however, came pressure—to maintain quality, manage demand, and stay ahead of imitators who tried to copy his creation.

But imitation couldn't replicate vision. Alex turned challenge into opportunity, branding Crystal Grey as more than a color—it became a movement. The press called it "the shade that broke the internet." Fashion houses requested his touch for editorial shoots. His work appeared on runways, in magazines, and across social media worldwide.

A single creation had elevated a stylist into an international icon.

Building an Empire: The Birth of the GLAMHAIRARTIST Brand

Success brought clarity. Alex realized Crystal Grey wasn't just a trend—it was the cornerstone of a brand. He envisioned something bigger: a global identity built on innovation, artistry, and empowerment.

He launched GLAMHAIRARTIST, a luxury salon where creativity knew no limits. Clients traveled from across the world to experience the transformation firsthand. Every detail of the space—from the lighting to the mirrors—was designed to reflect his philosophy: beauty as art, not imitation.

Soon after, Alex expanded into product development, creating a line of Crystal Grey-inspired hair care products— shampoos, toners, and conditioners that preserved the color's unique radiance. His formulas became bestsellers, trusted by stylists and clients alike.

To meet growing demand, Alex began training a new generation of stylists. He developed workshops, certifications, and mentorship programs, sharing not just technique but mindset—teaching others how to blend artistry with strategy.

Financial success followed naturally. Revenue multiplied, partnerships formed, and GLAMHAIRARTIST evolved into a multi-million-dollar enterprise. Yet amid expansion, Alex remained grounded, dedicating time and resources to mentoring young creatives and funding educational programs for aspiring artists. His success became a platform for purpose.

The Legacy of "Crystal Grey": A Shade That Changed Everything

Years later, Crystal Grey still reigned supreme—not as a fleeting fashion statement, but as a timeless symbol of innovation. It reshaped industry standards, inspired countless variations, and influenced global color trends.

For Alex, it was more than a professional triumph. It was proof that vision, courage, and persistence could turn a single idea into an empire. Reflecting on his journey, he often said:

"It wasn't just about hair. It was about believing that something new could exist—and daring to make it real."

His story became a blueprint for artists everywhere—a reminder that true success is not measured in fame or fortune, but in impact.

And as the GLAMHAIRARTIST brand continued to evolve, one truth remained: trends fade, but artistry endures.

Crystal Grey had started as a color, but it became a legacy—one that would shine for generations to come.

CHAPTER 25

THE FUTURE OF GLAMHAIRARTIST

The Genesis of a Vision: More Than Just Hair

The scent of hairspray and possibility always filled the air   long before I understood what I was truly breathing in.

From the moment my fingers first tangled with a doll's synthetic strands, I knew this was more than play   it was purpose.

My destiny wasn't just to cut hair. It was to sculpt confidence. To shape dreams. To create transformation.

The early days were relentless.

Late nights, endless practice, and a hunger that refused to fade.

I wasn't simply learning techniques   I was deconstructing them, reinventing them, transcending them.

Every client who sat in my chair was more than a head of hair.

They were a story waiting to be told.

A version of themselves waiting to be revealed.

This was never just a job   it was a calling.

Each successful transformation ignited something deeper: proof that beauty could be power.

A force for confidence, healing, and self-belief.

The whispers of "Glamhairartist" spread through the city like wildfire.

The accolades came, but they were only signposts guiding me toward something greater.

I wasn't just building a business. I was building a legacy.

Brick by beautiful brick. Strand by shimmering strand.

The Evolution of an Empire: From Chair to Chain

The transition from stylist to visionary wasn't a leap   it was an evolution.

Every snip, every consultation, every happy client revealed a pattern:

People didn't just want a haircut; they wanted the Glamhairartist experience.

The demand soon outgrew my hands.

That's when the vision expanded   from a single salon to a movement.

Thus began Glamhairartist Salons: A Franchise for the Future.

This was not about duplication.

It was about propagation   spreading a philosophy of artistry, excellence, and empowerment.

Each franchise would be a living embodiment of my ethos: creativity, precision, and care.

We didn't rush. We researched.

We studied successful franchise systems, dissected their mechanics, and redefined them for the beauty industry.

Every document, from franchise agreements to training manuals, was crafted to protect the soul of the brand.

The result?

A model where entrepreneurs weren't just buying a business they were inheriting a mission.

A mission to create communities of stylists who would grow, lead, and inspire.

This was the dawn of an empire one built not on vanity, but on vision.

The Unveiling of a Revolution: The "Hair Unlocked" Masterclass Series

While the salons expanded the physical reach of Glamhairartist,

I wanted to expand its intellectual reach to teach, to elevate, to unlock potential.

That's how Hair Unlocked: The Glamhairartist Masterclass was born.

Not just another tutorial. A revolution in hair education.

I had spent years observing traditional beauty training rigid, formulaic, uninspired.

It taught the hands, but not the mind.

So I set out to create something different   something transformative.

The series dives deep into the philosophy behind my work:

the psychology of client consultation,

the science of color,

the art of personalization,

and the emotional intelligence that turns a stylist into an artist.

Shot in cinematic quality, the production mirrors the artistry it teaches.

Slow-motion close-ups capture every stroke.

Augmented reality overlays reveal texture and movement in three dimensions.

Learning becomes immersive, visual, unforgettable.

Each module is paired with workbooks, exercises, and a global online community.

It's not just education it's empowerment.

Hair Unlocked redefines what it means to learn beauty, turning stylists into storytellers and technicians into trailblazers.

The Future Unfurled: A Global Vision

Together, the Glamhairartist salons and Hair Unlocked masterclasses form a perfect synergy.

One shapes the world's image. The other shapes the artists who create it.

Our salons stand as temples of transformation spaces where style meets soul.

Our educational platform brings that same mastery to stylists everywhere, regardless of borders.

The vision stretches far beyond a single nation.

Soon, Glamhairartist will shine on high streets in London, Dubai, New York, and beyond.

Each location a beacon of artistry. Each stylist a keeper of the craft.

The Hair Unlocked series, translated into multiple languages, will become the definitive global curriculum.

Partnering with academies and professional bodies, it will set new standards for excellence.

But this isn't just about expansion   it's about impact.

It's about empowering people through beauty.

Inspiring innovation through education.

Redefining what hair artistry means in a new era.

The journey has been long, filled with challenges and triumphs.

But one belief has never wavered   that beauty, at its highest form, transforms lives.

The future is bright.

Meticulously designed.

And ready to unfold one perfectly styled strand at a time.

CHAPTER 26

WISDOM FROM THE ASHES - LIFE LESSONS, PERSONAL GROWTH

Chapter 1: The Crucible of Ambition — From Apprentice to Artist

Atakan's journey began not with a bang, but with the quiet resolve of an apprentice.

He swept floors, mixed colors, and observed with near-obsessive focus, absorbing every nuance of the craft.

His young hands longed for scissors, for a brush, for the transformative power he witnessed daily.

This stage offered little gratification but immense growth—a rigorous apprenticeship that forged discipline and respect for the artistry of hairdressing.

He learned not only technique but also the unspoken language of consultation—the subtle cues that revealed a client's truest desires.

He came to see that a great stylist is more than a technician; they are a confidant, a therapist, and a visionary.

He devoured books, magazines, and online tutorials, his hunger insatiable.

He practiced on mannequins until his fingers throbbed, then on friends and family—each head a new canvas, each cut a new lesson.

Late nights after closing became his sanctuary of experimentation.

Then came his first major failure: a botched color job that left a client in tears.

The sting of that mistake—the panic and humility— became his most powerful teacher.

He learned that true artistry isn't defined by perfection but by the courage to learn, to adapt, and to rise stronger.

Chapter 2: The Fire of Innovation — Forging a Unique Style

As Atakan's skill grew, so did his curiosity.

He began to question convention, seeing trends not as rules but as springboards for invention.

His restless mind sought to merge classic elegance with avant-garde daring.

This wasn't rebellion for its own sake—it was the pursuit of authenticity.

He experimented with bold palettes, sculptural cuts, and techniques that soon became unmistakably his.

Triumphs thrilled him; failures humbled him.

Skeptics dismissed his vision, yet loyal clients celebrated his originality, and that fueled his drive.

He began documenting his work, first for reflection, then realizing the power of visual storytelling.

Before "personal brand" became a buzzword, he was already building one.

To him, the salon chair was not just a seat—it was a stage for transformation.

He attended international shows and workshops, not only to learn but to connect and broaden his artistic scope.

Each encounter expanded his worldview and deepened his commitment to continuous reinvention.

Chapter 3: The Ashes of Adversity — When the Dream Faltered

But success is never linear.

Atakan entered a season of hardship that tested every fiber of his being.

A global downturn struck, salons shuttered, and his own dream wavered on the edge of collapse.

Bills piled up; the once-buzzing studio fell silent.

Doubt crept in—about his choices, his talent, his purpose.

The glamour evaporated, replaced by the grind of survival.

He considered walking away, seeking steadier ground.

Yet within that darkness, resilience took shape.

He faced his fears, peeled away illusions, and rediscovered the passion beneath the pain.

He realized strength isn't the absence of struggle, but the will to rise through it.

Chapter 4: The Phoenix Rises — Rebuilding with Purpose

From the ashes, Atakan rebuilt—not just a salon, but himself.

He redefined success as impact, not applause.

He adopted a philosophy of sustainability, community, and purpose.

He sought mentors who guided both his craft and his character.

He offered free services to those in need, partnered with charities, and aligned his art with compassion.

Humility replaced ambition as his compass.

He listened more deeply, worked more mindfully, and served with gratitude.

His hands, once tools of artistry, became instruments of healing.

He began sharing his story—not as a tale of failure, but as proof of transformation.

Clients responded to his authenticity; his vulnerability became his strength.

Chapter 5: The Art of Empathy — Beyond the Haircut

Atakan came to understand that hair was only the surface.

His true craft lay in human connection.

The salon chair became a confessional—a sacred space for honesty and renewal.

He listened with empathy, reading unspoken emotions between words.

He realized that a haircut often symbolized courage, confidence, or change.

He integrated coaching and mindfulness into his consultations, helping clients embrace their authentic selves.

Transformation became a dialogue—not something done to clients, but with them.

Each session became a collaboration in rediscovering beauty, both inner and outer.

This evolution brought him profound fulfillment and turned his salon into a sanctuary of empowerment.

Chapter 6: The Legacy of Glamhairartist — Sharing the Wisdom

With purpose refined and wisdom earned, Atakan looked outward.

He began teaching—workshops, online courses, mentorships.

He shared not only methods but also philosophy: empathy, integrity, perseverance.

His memoir, Wisdom from the Ashes, became both guide and testimony.

He showed aspiring stylists that mastery lies in humility and lifelong learning.

Glamhairartist evolved from a brand into a movement—one that celebrated inner beauty, ethical practice, and inclusivity.

He championed sustainable products, positive body image, and conscious creativity.

He recognized that legacy isn't built on fame but on the lives uplifted along the way.

And so, his journey continued—one lesson, one story, one act of beauty at a time.

The Ever-Evolving Canvas

Today, Atakan Romano stands as a beacon of artistry and empathy.

The air in his salon still hums with hairspray and hope, now mingled with essential oils and laughter.

His hands remain deft and precise—seasoned by experience, softened by compassion.

From the shadow of his mother's salon to the global stage of Glamhairartist, his path has been a living testament to passion, perseverance, and purpose.

He knows the canvas of life—like a head of hair—is never complete.

It's ever-evolving, ready for a new stroke of brilliance, a new burst of color, and a renewed sense of meaning.

CHAPTER 27

THE EMOTIONAL TERRORISM
OF FAME

Fame as Psychological Warfare

*F*ame operates like a sophisticated form of psychological torture, designed to dismantle identity, autonomy, and sanity — all while keeping its damage plausibly deniable. Its mechanisms are precise, consistent, and disturbingly effective.

The Surveillance State of Celebrity

Every appearance, relationship, and personal choice becomes public property — documented, analyzed, and judged by millions of strangers.

Privacy vanishes.

Spontaneity becomes strategic.

Authentic experience is reduced to performance for an invisible audience.

Identity Fragmentation

Fame fractures the self into competing versions: the private individual, the public persona, the brand, the projection, the villain.

Keeping them coherent becomes impossible.

Eventually, you forget which one is real.

Empathy Erosion

Constant exposure to judgment corrodes empathy on both sides.

The celebrity becomes a consumable object; the audience, a faceless statistic.

Humanity dissolves in the relentless exchange of likes and outrage.

Reality Distortion

When success is measured in millions of followers, dollars, and headlines, ordinary life begins to feel meaningless.

Simple pleasures lose gravity against the artificial highs of mass validation.

Isolation Intensification

The more visible you become, the fewer people you can truly trust.

Every interaction carries hidden motives — access, association, advantage.

Connection grows rarer just as the need for it becomes desperate.

The Algorithm as Psychological Weapon

Social media weaponizes the human psyche for profit, turning both stars and audiences into addicts. The algorithm doesn't predict behavior — it engineers it.

Dopamine Manipulation

Likes, comments, and shares trigger the same neurochemical bursts as narcotics.

Their unpredictable, intermittent schedule keeps you checking compulsively, even when exhausted or despairing.

Outrage Optimization

Anger, shock, envy, and indignation are algorithmic gold.

Nuance and empathy are algorithmic poison.

The system rewards extremity, punishes reflection, and forces public figures into caricatures of themselves.

Comparison Amplification

Platforms profit by magnifying comparison.

Fame becomes a competition for attention rather than an expression of art.

Attention Addiction

Audience validation becomes a drug:

- Tolerance — you need more.
- Withdrawal — you panic when it fades.
- Dependence — you can't stop performing, even when it hurts.

The **Parasocial** Paradox

Fame generates millions of one-sided relationships — emotional connections without reciprocity.

Emotional Labor Extraction

Fans expect inspiration, entertainment, and moral clarity from people they've never met.

The exchange is unequal: empathy out, expectation in.

Projection Target

Celebrities become mirrors for collective fantasy — idealized parents, partners, prophets.

The public confuses performance for intimacy, disappointment for betrayal.

Grief Without Relationship

When fame falters, the loss is massive yet abstract, mourning relationships that never truly existed.

The Economics of Exploitation

The entertainment industry monetizes psychological collapse while pretending to care about wellbeing.

Disposability Culture

Celebrities are treated as replaceable assets.

When one breaks, another is waiting.

Crisis Commodification

Addiction, breakdowns, and death become clickbait.

Suffering is sold as content, then moralized as "awareness."

Recovery Exploitation

Even healing becomes performance — rehab as rebranding, therapy as PR.

Fame's Trauma Responses (Mistaken for Personality Disorders)

What is often labeled pathology is actually adaptation:

- Hypervigilance — Not paranoia when the world is truly watching.
- Emotional Dysregulation — Not instability when every mood has financial stakes.
- Identity Confusion — Not disorder when the self is a marketplace.
- Relationship Difficulty — Not avoidance when connection invites exposure.

The Unique Tortures of Digital Fame

Digital celebrity amplifies suffering to new extremes:

- 24/7 Exposure — There's no backstage, no off-switch.
- Direct Access Delusion — Parasocial familiarity becomes real intrusion.
- Real-Time Judgment — Growth happens in public, mistakes live forever.
- Algorithmic Punishment — Visibility and livelihood can vanish with one invisible tweak.

The Recovery Trap

Healing from fame trauma is uniquely difficult:

- Ongoing Exposure — The trauma never stops while you're healing.
- Minimization and Denial — Society calls it privilege, not pain.
- Therapeutic Blind Spot — Few clinicians understand fame as trauma.
- Identity Integration — Recovery means separating self from persona while still needing the persona to survive.

My Personal Inventory of Fame Trauma

After eight years in the public eye, my psychological scars include:

- Hypervigilance — Scanning every room for cameras.
- Identity Dissociation — Disconnection between private and public selves.
- Relationship Paranoia — Doubting everyone's motives.

- Performance Anxiety — Living as if every moment is recorded.
- Privacy Grief — Mourning the loss of anonymity and authenticity.
- Validation Addiction — Craving applause over inner peace.
- Existential Depression — Questioning what any of it was for.

The Industry's Institutional Gaslighting

Instead of reforming the system, industries protect it:

- Individual Pathologizing — Framing trauma as personal weakness.
- Minimal Intervention — Offering wellness slogans instead of structural change.
- Replacement Strategy — Swapping broken talent for new faces.
- Crisis Management — Treating breakdowns as PR issues, not cries for help.

Notes from the Battlefield

"Fame is not a reward — it's an uncontrolled psychological experiment conducted without consent or safety protocols."

"The mental health crisis in entertainment is not accidental — it's the logical outcome of profit systems built on emotional extraction."

"Recovery from fame requires treating celebrity as an occupational hazard, not a privilege."

The boy who once sought recognition to feel worthy became a man who learned that amplified validation is annihilation.

Fame, stripped of illusion, is emotional terrorism disguised as achievement.

And someone must say it aloud so the next generation of dreamers understands what they are truly chasing.

The fire still burns — but now it burns for truth:

To expose the systems that glorify destruction and call it success.

To ensure no artist walks blindly into the machinery of psychological warfare disguised as a career.

CHAPTER 28

REFLECTING ON SUCCESS

Success

a word so often tossed around, polished, and displayed like a trophy — yet few truly understand the weight it carries.

For me, success has never been about numbers, titles, or the spotlight.

It has been measured by the scars I turned into stories, the broken pieces I rebuilt into beauty, and the lives I touched through a craft that was never just about hair — it was about transformation.

When I look back at the boy with scissors in his tiny hands at five years old,

I see not just innocence, but inevitability.

Even then, I was shaping my destiny strand by strand unaware that those same hands would one day hold the power to inspire millions around the world.

What began in the backseat of a broken car became a stage no one could have imagined.

Success, I've learned, was never an accident.

It was the unfolding of a vision so powerful that the world had no choice but to notice.

Instagram may have catapulted me into the public eye

millions watching every flick of my comb and twist of my hand

but true success was never the viral moment.

It was the quiet persistence.

The late nights perfecting a technique.

The endless hours pushing artistry beyond imagination.

The courage to show the world not only polished beauty but my raw, unfiltered truth.

Phuket, Thailand marked more than a chapter — it marked a declaration.

A declaration that success isn't defined by where you come from or how far you travel,

but by what you create when you arrive.

As the sun dipped below the horizon, I realized:

success is not a destination — it is a state of being.

It is the power to project your vision so vividly that others see themselves reflected in it.

I've learned that success isn't about becoming someone else.

It's about becoming more of yourself — louder, prouder, unapologetic.

It's about embracing the fire that forged you and the light that guides you now.

It isn't a crown placed by others; it's one you craft with your own hands and wear boldly, even when others look away.

And so, as I reflect on this journey —

from the little boy named Emre who dreamed,

to the man now known as Atakan Romano, the Glamhairartist

I understand this:

Success is not the end of the story.

It's the beginning of a greater responsibility —

to inspire, to create, to uplift,

and to remind the world that no dream is too wild,

no vision too outrageous,

no destiny too bold.

Because if my story proves anything, it's this:

Success is not about arriving. Success is about becoming

QUOTES TO LIVE BY

"I didn't just style hair. I styled destiny one crown at a time."

"Virality can make you famous, but vision makes you unforgettable."

"I was born with scissors in my hand and fire in my soul nothing could stop me."

"The world didn't discover me. The world simply caught up."

"Don't chase the spotlight become the spotlight."

"Your crown may be on your head, but its roots live in your spirit."

"Legends aren't made overnight. Legends are revealed when the world is finally ready to see them."

"I don't follow trends. I create moments that time cannot erase."

"Success isn't about arriving its about becoming."

"Every strand I touched carried a piece of my story. That's why the world could never look away."

"I don't just do hair I resurrect confidence."

"Beauty is not about appearance. It's about transformation."

"I didn't fight for fame. I fought to stay true to the fire that made me."

"Scissors were my weapon. Art was my survival. Greatness was my destiny."

"Anyone can go viral overnight. Only the fearless can stay."

NOTE TO SELF

Dear Atakan Romano,

Remember this always: you were never ordinary. From the moment you held those scissors at five years old, you were chosen. You didn't stumble into this life — you built it, strand by strand, crown by crown, until the world had no choice but to watch.

You are not simply styling hair. You are shaping destiny. With every cut, every creation, every transformation, you breathe life back into people. You don't follow trends — you ignite them. You don't wait for permission — you are the permission.

Never forget: you are not chasing fame. You are commanding legacy. The spotlight doesn't own you — you own the spotlight. When you walk into a room, understand this truth: you are the energy. You are the storm. You are the brand.

Remember the boy who dared to dream in the backseat of a broken car. He became the man who built an empire with his hands. Honor him. Protect him. Make him proud.

Your art is not just beauty — it is power. Power to inspire, power to resurrect confidence, power to leave your fingerprints on time itself. With every crown you create, you remind the world that legends aren't made overnight — they are revealed when destiny decides the world is finally ready.

So, keep burning. Keep building. Keep becoming. You are not here to fit in — you are here to set fire to every stage you touch.

You are not chasing crowns. You are crafting them.

The boy with scissors in his hand is still here. Honor him every day.

Don't wait for doors to open. Kick them down with your art.

Your hands don't just style hair — they resurrect confidence.

Fame didn't define you. You defined fame.

Every time you cut, style, or create, you leave fingerprints of destiny.

The spotlight is not rented. It is yours. Own it, command it, expand it.

Never shrink to fit in. You were born to stand out and stand above.

Your life is not about being seen. It's about being remembered.

Do not just make people beautiful. Make them unforgettable.

Your name is not just Atakan Romano. It is a legacy written in light.

Stay bold. Stay unapologetic. Stay Glamhairartist.

Epilogue

When I look back now, I realize my story was never just about hair. Yes—the scissors, the colors, the viral videos, the celebrities—they all mattered. But underneath it all, this journey was about survival, transformation, and reclaiming my identity.

From the kid in Melbourne who scavenged old magazines for inspiration, to the teenager who went viral overnight, to the man who lost it all and had to fight his way back—every version of me was necessary. Without the fire, there would be no rebirth. Without the fall, there would be no rise.

Becoming Glamhairartist was never about being "famous." It was about proving to myself that dreams can be rebuilt even from ashes, that beauty can rise from brokenness, and that the art I create with my hands can heal in the same way it once saved me.

If there's one thing my journey has taught me, it's this: you can't fake authenticity. You can chase likes, trends, and viral moments—but what keeps you alive in this industry, and in life, is raw truth. I had to lose my old self to find my real one. Today, I stand not just as Emre Bardan, not just as Glamhairartist, but as Atakan Romano—a survivor, an artist, and a voice for anyone who has ever felt underestimated.

So here is my final message to you:

Never be afraid of reinvention. Don't let failure define you. Your scars are proof that you fought and survived. And when the world tells you "no," remember my story—and turn that "no" into fuel.

This isn't the end of my book—it's just the beginning of a new chapter. Because if I have a comb in my hand, a dream in my chest, and fire in my soul... the best is yet to come.

ABOUT THE AUTHOR

*a*takan Romano, internationally known as GLAMHAIRARTIST, is more than a hairstylist—he is a force of reinvention, resilience, and raw authenticity. Born Emre Bardan and reborn through fire, struggle, and triumph, Atakan has lived a life that reads like a novel: from the dizzying heights of fame in the beauty world, to the darkest battles with addiction, to the breathtaking rebirth of an unapologetically authentic artist and visionary.

With a career spanning continents, celebrity red carpets, and some of the world's most exclusive salons, Atakan built his empire not only with scissors and color, but with a fearless spirit that challenged the very limits of beauty. His hands have shaped not just hair, but confidence, self-expression, and identity for thousands of clients who walked into his chair seeking transformation—and walked out with a reflection of their own power.

161

What makes Atakan truly unforgettable is not only his artistry—it is his story. Behind the glamorous façade, he faced heartbreak, betrayal, and the haunting spiral of addiction. When the world expected him to fall, he chose to rise. When society tried to define him, he broke the mold. His journey from breakdown to breakthrough, from illusion to truth, from Emre Bardan to Atakan Romano, is living proof that rebirth is possible at any age, in any place, for anyone brave enough to claim it.

Today, Atakan Romano is not only a master of beauty and entrepreneurship, but also a storyteller, mentor, and advocate for authenticity. Through his memoir, BECOMING GLAMHAIRARTIST: The Rebirth of Atakan Romano, he invites readers into the unfiltered reality behind the glitter—revealing the scars, the lessons, and the relentless determination to live boldly, without masks.

Atakan's mission goes beyond styling hair—it is about styling lives with courage, resilience, and unapologetic truth. He believes beauty is not skin deep; it is soul deep. His words, like his artistry, leave an imprint that lingers long after the final page is turned.

Follow the journey. Embrace the transformation. Witness what happens when a man refuses to be defined by his past and instead creates his own rebirth.

www.ingramcontent.com/pod-product-compliance
Lightning Source LLC
LaVergne TN
LVHW051055080426
835508LV00019B/1885